HE WAS AND IS AND ALWAYS WILL BE

HE WAS AND IS AND ALWAYS WILL BE

OLD TESTAMENT PROPHECIES FULFILLED

BY
BILL PRICE

RESOURCE *Publications* • Eugene, Oregon

HE WAS AND IS AND ALWAYS WILL BE
Old Testament Prophecies Fulfilled

Resource Publications
An Imprint of Wipf and Stock Publishers
199 W. 8th Ave., Suite 3
Eugene, OR 97401

www.wipfandstock.com

PAPERBACK ISBN: 979-8-3852-3942-9
HARDCOVER ISBN: 979-8-3852-3943-6
EBOOK ISBN: 979-8-3852-3944-3
VERSION NUMBER 01/28/25

To Mom—who gave me my first glimpse of God's love.

THE REVELATION 1:8

I am the *Alpha and the Omega*, saith the Lord God,
who is and who was
and who is to come, the Almighty.

ISAIAH 9:6

For to us a child is born, to us a son is given; and the government
shall be upon his shoulder,
and his name shall be called Wonderful Counselor, Mighty God,
Everlasting Father, Prince of Peace.

CONTENTS

Chapter 1   PROPHECIES | 1

Chapter 2   WHAT ARE THE ODDS? | 8

Chapter 3   BIRTH: THE PROPHECIES AND THEIR FULFILLMENT | 13

Chapter 4   PROPHECIES OF THE NATURE OF JESUS | 18

Chapter 5   PROPHESIED LIFE OF THE SON OF GOD | 25

Chapter 6   PROPHESIED DEATH OF A SON | 34

Chapter 7   AFTER THE RESURRECTION | 44

Chapter 8   THE ASCENSION | 51

Chapter 9   ATONEMENT | 56

Chapter 10   JESUS DEFINED AS GOD | 60

Chapter 11   HE IS COMING AGAIN | 67

Chapter 12   "COME UP HERE" | 72

Chapter 13   TRIBULATION AND THE ANTICHRIST | 78

Chapter 14   "WORTHY IS THE LAMB" | 83

Chapter 15   SEVEN BOWLS OF JUDGMENT | 96

Chapter 16   A NEW HEAVEN AND A NEW EARTH | 102

Chapter 17   FINALE | 111

Appendix   THE APOSTLES—GAVE THEIR LIVES FOR JESUS | 115

BIBLIOGRAPHY | 119

Chapter 1

PROPHECIES

MY SEARCH FOR THE MEANING of my life was filled with both joys and disappointments. I have always stated that every man and every woman goes through a time when he or she questions why he or she has been born and what purpose he or she has on this plane of existence. My book called *My Search* was written to explain how I found that the reason for my existence was to serve God and prove that his Son, Jesus (Yeshua), was the Christ. It wasn't always that way, of course. Before I found a life serving Jesus, I was the type of person who had been brought up in a church family, and I knew the stories taught in Sunday School and in books read to me by my mother. I knew that all people, since the fall of Adam, had been born into sin and had lived in sin and I was one of them. I just thought that if God was really love, I would be just fine; besides, I was young and had plenty of time to accept Jesus when I was older. That choice, in itself, led to a less than happy life.

My life, like many others, was filled with disappointments because I depended on others to satisfy my needs. I was living for me and I didn't care about anyone else. I always said I did care about others, but I was just lying to myself. My concerns were to fulfill any of my desires to help fill a void in me. It didn't matter whether it was a need for food, for love, or for money. I was living for myself and myself alone. If I hurt someone, well that was just a consequence I was willing to live with. I had always heard "life is short, get the best out of it." I never considered what would happen to me if there was a catastrophic event that would end my life before my old age.

When I started thinking about the events that would occur if I suddenly died, I was filled with fear. I had heard the quotes from the Bible about eternal life, whether it was to consist of a "foreverness" with the King of kings or was to be taken to an eternity of hell-fire and brimstone with the torments of Satan. I had read about the devil and the place where he was bound for, after the Messiah returned with his heavenly kingdom, down to earth. As a student of literature I knew of the hell described by Dante in his *The Inferno*. This place was where Dante's character was led by Virgil through hell, where he saw nine circles of torment. Each level, or circle, was the degree of torment suffered by people who had rejected Jesus and spiritual values. Each level was worse than the last, and one was placed in a specific level according to the sins committed during his or her life. The Bible, in Rev 20:13–15, however, explains that "death and Hades gave up the dead that were in them, and each person was judged according to what they had done. Then death and Hades were thrown into the lake of fire. The lake of fire is the second death. Anyone whose name was not found written in the book of life was thrown into the lake of fire." Because of the way I had lived, I knew that there was no way my name would be written in the book of life.

I also knew, from my youth, that the choice of heaven or hell was my choice. Heaven was a place where "God will wipe away every tear from their eyes; there shall be no more death, nor sorrow, nor crying. There shall be no more pain, for the former things have passed away" (Rev 21:4). Those whose name had been written in the Book of Life would enjoy eternity with the King of kings, the Messiah, the Savior of the world. In John 5:24, Jesus said, "Whoever hears my word and believes him who sent me has eternal life and will not be judged but has crossed over from death to life."

I did decide to follow the teachings of Jesus and found out that he was who he said he was. It was then that I discovered what joy was. I knew that even though I was still a sinner and that I failed Jesus many times, even though I could become angry or depressed, I could ask for his help and receive it, and I could request forgiveness and start again trying to live for him. I knew I had to be sincere and also knew that it would be a daily struggle, but I accepted the challenge. It's hard to understand that salvation is ours simply by accepting Jesus as the Son of God, asking forgiveness for our sins, and by following his example of love. I realized that I could never make it by my works. It had to be because of my faith. Ephesians 2:8–9 tells us, "For by grace you have been saved through faith, and that not of yourselves; it is the gift of God, not of works, lest anyone should boast."

I knew after my first book, *My Search*, I had found the purpose for which I was born. I chose to follow the Christ. I did, however, know that I must go on another search that would require me to study the Bible and find answers in the New Testament that were backed up by verses found in the Old Testament and the Torah, even if it meant studying meanings of words translated from the Greek and the Hebrew. I decided to begin by researching how many prophecies from the Old Testament were fulfilled by Jesus during his lifetime.

I looked up the definition of prophecies first. In the Bible, "biblical prophecy" is a term used to describe passages that are communications from God to human beings through his prophets and only his prophets. Christians believe that biblical prophets received the words directly from God. If a prophecy was from God it would line up with the word of God, meaning it will either foretell, as Isaiah did in Isa 7:14, or forth-tell, as Elijah did in 1 Kgs 17:1–7. In other words, you could sum it up by stating that forth-telling is proclaiming and foretelling is predicting.

Isaiah foretold the people of Israel that "the Lord himself shall give you a sign: the maiden is with child and she will bear a son, and will call his name Immanuel" (Isa 7:14). His prophecies were concerned with the future. As a matter of fact, hundred of years in the future, God told his people that he was going to send them a Messiah who would fulfill the need to forgive sin and achieve eternal life. This Immanuel would come, but no one knew the day or the time that this would happen. However, it would happen because God said it would.

Elijah, on the other hand, proclaimed to Ahab that God was going to cause a drought.

> And Elijah the Tishbite, of the inhabitants of Gilead, said to Ahab, "As the Lord God of Israel lives, before whom I stand, there shall not be dew nor rain these years, except at my word." Then the word of the Lord came to him, saying, "Get away from here and turn eastward, and hide by the Brook Cherith, which flows into the Jordan. And it will be that you shall drink from the brook, and I have commanded the ravens to feed you there." So he went and did according to the word of the Lord, for he stayed by the Brook Cherith, which flows into the Jordan. The ravens brought him bread and meat in the morning, and bread and meat in the evening; and he drank from the brook. (1 Kgs 17:1–6)

His prophecies dealt with he immediate future. The drought was going to happen and it was to be imminent.

Prophets foretell or forth-tell, but how can anyone know that the prophecy is actually from God? How do we know if someone is speaking for the Lord or is merely suggesting something for fame or fortune? Just suppose that person is actually speaking for other gods, and not the King of kings? Deuteronomy 18:20 explains it well by stating: "But if a prophet presumes to speak a word in my name that I have not commanded, or speaks in the name of other gods, that prophet shall die." We know, though, that all humans will die eventually, so there have to be other ways to accept that a prophecy is indeed from God.

There have been many "prophets" who claim they know the voice of God. For example, preacher William Miller, in 1843, proclaimed that "the end of the world as we know it would occur with the second coming of Jesus Christ in 1843." This man had a following of over one hundred thousand people who actually believed they were soon going to be raptured to heaven. On New Years Day 1844, Miller recalculated his prediction and stated he was merely one year off. At the end of that year, one of his followers, Henry Emmons, wrote, "I waited all Tuesday, and dear Jesus did not come . . . I lay prostrate for 2 days without any pain—sick with disappointment."[1] Of course Miller has since passed away, but people soon realized he was a false prophet.

A *Britannica* publication composed the following.

> Taiwanese religious leader Hon-Ming Chen established Chen Tao, or True Way, a religious movement that blended elements of Christianity, Buddhism, UFO conspiracy theories, and Taiwanese folk religion. Chen preached that God would appear on U.S. television channel 18 on March 25, 1988, to announce that he would descend to Earth the following week in a physical form identical to Chen. The following year, he prophesied, millions of devil spirits, together with massive flooding, would result in a mass extinction of the human population. Followers could be spared by buying their way aboard spaceships, disguised as clouds, sent to rescue them.[2]

People waited and nothing happened.

1. Cole, "10 Failed Doomsday Predictions."
2. Cole, "10 Failed Doomsday Predictions."

In the paper *Edmond Life and Leisure* an article is found describing many false prophets. The article's author claims:

> Among the most prolific modern predictors of end times, Harold Camping has publicly predicted the end of the world as many as 12 times based his interpretations of biblical numerology. In 1992, he published a book, ominously titled *1994?*, which predicted the end of the world sometime around that year. Perhaps his most high-profile predication was for May 21, 2011, a date that he calculated to be exactly 7,000 years after the biblical flood. When that date passed without incident, he declared his math to be off and pushed back the end of the world to October 21, 2011.[3]

Yes, the penalty for a false prophet, including someone speaking in the name of a god other than YHWH (the name of God in Hebrew) or speaking arrogantly in Yahweh's name, according to Deut 18:20—is death. So, how do we know a prophecy comes from the Lord? How do we discern whether someone is speaking a message from God? To avoid false prophets, there are ways to test to see if a person has received a message and is conveying that message to us from the Almighty. I think the first thing one must do is to make sure the prophecy lines up with biblical scripture. 1 John 4:1–3 explains that we should test the prophet. John writes, "Beloved, do not believe every spirit, but test the spirits to see whether they are from God, for many false prophets have gone out into the world. By this you know the Spirit of God: every spirit that confesses that Jesus Christ has come in the flesh is from God, and every spirit that does not confess Jesus is not from God. This is the spirit of the Antichrist, which you heard was coming and now is in the world already." Paul, too, discussed prophecy when he wrote to the Thessalonians. He said, "Do not despise prophecies, but test everything; hold fast what is good" (1 Thess 5:20–21). Even Prov 30:5–6 says, "Every word of God is tested; He is a shield to those who take refuge in Him. Do not add to His words or He will reprove you, and you will be proved a liar." Do not, ever, take someone's word that they have received a message from God, unless it is biblical.

Next, if what a prophet has said could possibly be found in the Bible, then to identify it as a true word from God it must come true. God told the Hebrew people how to tell if a prophet was the real deal. The real prophet would not make mistakes, because if he was real the words would be of God, and God doesn't make mistakes. If the prophet spoke something that

---

3. Hibbard, "Predictions That Did Not Happen."

was not biblical, the Jewish people would know the speaker was a fraud. Deuteronomy 18:22 describes this best when it says, "When a prophet speaketh in the name of the Lord, if the thing follow not, nor come to pass, that is the thing which the Lord hath not spoken, but the prophet hath spoken it presumptuously: thou shalt not be afraid of him."

Matthew, in Matt 7:16–20, writes about the third test of prophecy. He writes, "By their fruits ye shall know them. Do men gather grapes of thorns, or figs of thistles? Even so every good tree bringeth forth good fruit; but the corrupt tree bringeth forth evil fruit. A good tree cannot bring forth evil fruit, neither can a corrupt tree bring forth good fruit. Every tree that bringeth not forth good fruit is hewn down, and cast into the fire. Therefore by their fruits ye shall know them." When he states this, he is explaining that the prophet must show the fruit of godly character. This fruit, or the fruits of the Spirit, contain nine qualities of a life guided by the Holy Spirit. A true prophet must possess these attributes: love, joy, peace, patience, kindness, faithfulness, gentleness, and self control. This, added to the two prior tests, pretty much assures that the words they are presenting are indeed true.

Just to be sure, though, test the prophet to make sure God has revealed himself to them. St. Peter explained that "no prophecy of the scripture is of any private interpretation. For the prophecy came not in old time by the will of man: but holy men of God spake as they were moved by the Holy Ghost" (2 Pet 1:20–21). If the message is only partly true, the message is not from God. This person has not received a revelation from God. If this message does not glorify God, if it does not follow his principles, than it is not a prophecy.

There are, however, prophecies found in the Old Testament that have been proved by all of these tests. These prophecies deal with the Messiah, the man who would be born and who would save the souls of everyone who accepts him. He would be a man, but he also was God. He would be the Savior of mankind.

In-depth research needed to be done to explain the old prophecies. I needed to find out who prophesied what and how the prophecy came to fruition. The New Testament Gospels explain the story of Jesus, the Christ, the Savior on earth. The prophecies of the Bible, particularly found in Daniel and Isaiah, are also found throughout the Old Testament and show us who the Messiah would be and what Jesus, as Savior, was saving us from and saving us to. His promise was to save us from hell, and he was saving us for eternal life with him in heaven.

PROPHECIES

The story of Jesus is found throughout the Bible, and the prophecies of who he would be are found throughout the Old Testament. Prophecies about him also told of events that he would be involved in and suggest the work he would do. The prophecies of old needed to be tested to see if they fulfill the definition. Were these prophets actually foretelling how God intended to save us from sin? Were they imparting actual information from God? Were they true, and did they really happen?

Chapter 2

WHAT ARE THE ODDS?

DEFINING THE ODDS OF a certain thing happening or not happening could be determined by using the laws of probability. If one wanted to flip a coin one hundred times to determine how many times the coin landed on heads, one could figure the probability of heads appearing. Since there are only two choices, heads or tails, and a fair and balanced coin is used, then the probability of the flip ending on heads is 0.5×100=50. How then could someone decide the probability of one man fulfilling all the Old Testament prophecies? First of all, the number of biblical prophecies must be determined.

Many scholars have tried to determine how many prophets foretold and how many prophecies were concerned with the Jewish Messiah. J. Barton Payne, author and scholar, has found as many as 574 verses. These verses come from the Old Testament and describe who the coming Messiah would be. The prophets showed exactly who would fulfill prophecy, who would be the awaited king, the promised deliverer of God's people, and the savior of the world. Payne wrote a guide to biblical prophecies that stemmed from Adam to God's new heaven on earth with Jesus as King. His book concerned itself with every prophecy in the Scriptures. It covered all prophesies that happened in the past, the ones that are occurring today, and those that have not come to fruition. This is the description of Payne's book:

> For example: The 12 verses of Genesis that foretell God's granting of the land of Canaan to the descendants of Abraham are discussed together. It is then shown how the promise was fulfilled in the days of Joshua. One of the ENCYCLOPEDIA'S concluding summaries lists all the 737 major subjects that appear in Biblical prediction,

with the books and paragraphs in which each is found. This way, each prophecy can be traced from its first appearance in the Bible to its last. Among the many features is a complete list of all the Scriptural prophecies pertaining to Christ. No other book has ever examined Biblical prophecy so thoroughly or presented it in such a balanced perspective as the ENCYCLOPEDIA OF BIBLICAL PROPHECY. The ENCYCLOPEDIA OF BIBLICAL PROPHECY is certain to bring a fresh understanding and rewarding insights of the Bible.[1]

Edgar F. Sanders, the director of the Biblical Research Institute, wrote, "This book is destined to become the standard work on Biblical eschatology [the part of theology concerned with death, judgment, and the final destiny of the soul and of humankind]. It is a very balanced and scholarly treatment from a devout evangelical who is committed to the inspired word of God."[2] Another author, Alfred Edersheim, was a Jewish author and scholar who wrote about the traditions of the Jewish faith and life of Christ. He found 456 Old Testament verses, not necessarily prophesying but definitely referring to the Messiah or his times. Edersheim wrote, "The most important point here is to keep in mind the organic unity of the Old Testament. Its predictions are not isolated, but features of one grand prophetic picture; its ritual and institutions parts of one great system; its history, not loosely connected events, but an organic development tending towards a definite end."[3] In other words, the Old Testament is unified in its predictions of who the Messiah would be and what he would do.

Eugene J. Mayhew, professor of Old Testament and Semitic languages at Moody Theological Seminary, wrote, "The written labors of Alfred Edersheim have had a profound impact on Bible teachers for over a century; however, his personal life has been shrouded in obscurity. A Jewish convert to true biblical Christianity, he now stands as one of the foremost Hebrew Christian scholars in the history of the Church."[4] These authors, continually used for Bible research, have been trustworthy in that what they have written lends proof to the biblical prophecies and a factual understanding of the prophesied Messiah.

1. *Theologue*, "Encyclopedia of Biblical Prophecy."
2. *Theologue*, "Encyclopedia of Biblical Prophecy."
3. Bible Hub, "What Messiah."
4. Mayhew, "Alfred Edersheim."

Payne and Edersheim found over 500 prophecies, but, for the sake of argument, let's use a conservative number to determine how Jesus fulfilled at least 300 prophecies in his earthly ministry. First, though, let's look at the mathematical probability of one man fulfilling only eight of the Old Testament verses. Professor Peter Stoner conducted mathematical experiments using probability to determine the odds of one man fulfilling all of the messianic prophecies. In his book *Science Speaks*, Stoner decided to take only eight prophecies. He made sure that his calculations were on the conservative side.[5]

The first prophecy came from Mic 5:2, which predicted the Messiah would be born in Bethlehem. He wrote, "The average population of Bethlehem from the time of Micah to the present (1958) divided by the average population of the earth during the same period=7,150/2,000,000,000 or 2.8×10^5."[6]

Next, he looked at Mal 3:1, which says, "'I will send my messenger, who will prepare the way before me. Then suddenly the Lord you are seeking will come to his temple; the messenger of the covenant, whom you desire, will come,' says the LORD Almighty." Stoner wrote, "One man in how many, the world over, has had a forerunner (in this case, John the Baptist) to prepare his way? Estimate: 1 in 1,000 or 1×10^3." The professor continued by using Zech 9:9: "Rejoice greatly, Daughter Zion! Shout, Daughter Jerusalem! See, your king comes to you, righteous and victorious, lowly and riding on a donkey, on a colt, the foal of a donkey." Jesus entered Jerusalem with the crowds shouting that he was the King of the Jews. Stoner's estimate: 1 in 100 or 1×10^2.

Zechariah 13:6 describes that the Messiah would be betrayed by a friend and explains the wounds found on the hands of the crucified Christ. Peter Stoner continues by writing, "One man in how many, the world over, has been betrayed by a friend, resulting in wounds in his hands? Estimate: 1 in 1,000 or 1×10^3." These first four alone show the odds of Jesus being the savior of his people, but this professor continued.

The author found the verse in Zech 11:12, that the Messiah would be betrayed for thirty pieces of silver. Matthew 26:14–16 tells us, "Then one of the Twelve—the one called Judas Iscariot—went to the chief priests and asked, 'What are you willing to give me if I deliver him over to you?' So they

5. Bible.org, "Probability of Prophecies Fulfilled."

6. Reagan, "Applying the Science of Probability." All the following calculations cited are found in Reagan's summary article of Stoner's work.

counted out for him thirty pieces of silver. From then on Judas watched for an opportunity to hand him over." Stoner calculated that "of the people who have been betrayed, one in how many has been betrayed for exactly 30 pieces of silver? Estimate: 1 in 1,000 or 1×10^3."

The sixth example was found when Zechariah spoke saying, "And the Lord said to me, 'Throw it to the potter'—the handsome price at which they valued me! So I took the thirty pieces of silver and threw them to the potter at the house of the Lord" (Zech 11:13). "One man in how many, after receiving a bribe for the betrayal of a friend, has returned the money, had it refused, and then experienced it being used to buy a potter's field? Estimate: 1 in 100,000 or 1×10^5," stated Stoner.

Peter Stoner found the next example in Isa 53:7, which states, "The Messiah will remain silent while He is afflicted." This college professor wrote, "One man in how many, when he is oppressed and afflicted, though innocent, will make no defense of himself? Estimate: 1 in 1,000 or 1×10^3." The final and eighth example Stoner wrote of concerned itself with the Messiah who would die by having his hands and feet pierced. This verse is found in Ps 22:16. One man out of how many would be killed in this manner? The estimate was 1 in 10,000 or 1×10^4.

So what was Stoner's final calculation? Stoner found "multiplying all these probabilities together produces a number (rounded off) of 1×10^{28}. Dividing this number by an estimate of the number of people who have lived since the time of these prophecies (88 billion) produces a probability of all 8 prophecies being fulfilled accidentally in the life of one person. That probability is 1 in 10^{17} or 1 in 100,000,000,000,000,000. That's one in one hundred quadrillion!"[7]

Professor Peter Stoner, from Westmont College, also attempted to calculate the mathematical probability of one man fulfilling all of the prophecies dealing with the King of the Jews in the Old Testament. He utilized the help of six hundred students from twelve of his classes. They used only the most conservative estimates, making sure that they arrived at a mostly unanimous decision. The American Scientific Affiliation accepted his study and found that his and his students' calculations were credible from a scientific viewpoint. The results showed that the "most conservative estimate on the odds was one in ten to the 157th power; that's ten followed by 157 zeroes!"[8]

7. Reagan, "Applying the Science of Probability."
8. Schmidt, "Fulfilled."

Professor Peter Stoner stated, "Any man who rejects Christ as the Son of God is rejecting a fact proved perhaps more absolutely than any other fact in the world."[9] These prophecies fulfilled by Jesus are so compelling that even Jesus recognized his place in prophecy. On the road to Emmaus, after his resurrection, Jesus met two of his disciples, possibly Cleopas and Mary. They did not recognize him until they invited him to have supper with them. When he broke bread, he handed it to them and their eyes were opened and they recognized him. They returned to Jerusalem and reunited with the other disciples.

They explained that they had seen the risen Jesus and broken bread with him. While they were talking, Jesus simply appeared to them saying, "Peace be with you." The followers of Jesus were filled with amazement when they realized their Messiah had risen from the dead. Jesus ate with them and them explained this: "This is what I told you while I was still with you: Everything must be fulfilled that is written about me in the Law of Moses, the Prophets, and the Psalms. Then he opened their minds so they could understand the Scriptures" (Luke 24:44–45).

Everything that was ever written in the Old Testament and in the Hebrew Scriptures came true. Jesus Christ was the Jewish Messiah. This is what our belief in the Christ is based on. It is our hope in our Savior, and there is one final prophecy left to be fulfilled—he is coming again.

9. Schmidt, "Fulfilled."

Chapter 3

BIRTH

The Prophecies and Their Fulfillment

STONER AND HIS STUDENTS have done the mathematical work. Now it's time to look at actual prophecies above and beyond those presented by the professor. We must examine the words of the Old Testament and compare them to the New Testament and how Jesus fulfilled them. There is neither time nor the paper to find every one of the possible 574 verses previously described by author J. Barton Payne. Many must be researched by you, the reader.

We have already discussed the birthplace of Jesus; his predecessor, John; his triumphant ride into Jerusalem; his betrayer, Judas; and the method by which they would kill the Christ. It is time to take a deep dive into the Scriptures to prove that Jesus is the Messiah, the Savior of our souls, and the King of kings who will one day return, defeat Satan, and rule the world.

Genesis 3:15 describes a curse that is focused on Satan. God promises to make enemies of Satan and Eve. He tells us that all of her offspring will continue to be an enemy of the devil throughout all generations. Eve's offspring includes all mankind, including the future son of Mary, the Christ Child. Moses explains, in Gen 3:15, "And I will put enmity between you and the woman, and between your offspring and hers; he will crush your head, and you will strike his heel." Hebrews 2:14 lets us know that "because God's children are human beings, made of flesh and blood, the Son [of God] also became flesh and blood. For only as a human being could he die, and only by dying could he break the power of the devil, who had the power of death." It was for that purpose Jesus was born.

To begin, Jesus was born of a virgin. Isaiah 7:14 stated that "therefore the Lord himself shall give you a sign: the maiden is with child and she will bear a son, and will call his name Immanuel." The New Testament according to Matthew begins with the genealogy of Jesus, which we will further investigate later. After that Matthew wrote:

> This is how the birth of Jesus the Messiah came about: His mother Mary was pledged to be married to Joseph, but before they came together, she was found to be pregnant through the Holy Spirit. Because Joseph her husband was faithful to the law, and yet did not want to expose her to public disgrace, he had in mind to divorce her quietly. But after he had considered this, an angel of the Lord appeared to him in a dream and said, "Joseph son of David, do not be afraid to take Mary home as your wife, because what is conceived in her is from the Holy Spirit. She will give birth to a son, and you are to give him the name Jesus, because he will save his people from their sins." All this took place to fulfill what the Lord had said through the prophet: "The virgin will conceive and give birth to a son, and they will call him Immanuel" (which means "God with us"). (Matt 1:18–23).

Psalm 2:7 explains that Jesus would be the son of God. I have called this the prophecy of the psalmist. The psalm proclaims the Lord's decree that he would have a son to save his people: "He said to me, 'You are my son; today I have become your father.'" Matthew told what happened after Jesus was baptized. Matthew chapter 3, verse 7, stated, "As soon as Jesus was baptized, he went up out of the water. At that moment heaven was opened, and he saw the Spirit of God descending like a dove and alighting on him. And a voice from heaven said, 'This is my Son, whom I love; with him I am well pleased.'"

Prophecy also declared the Messiah would be from the seed of Abraham. Genesis 12:3 discusses the promise God made to Abraham. "I will bless those who bless you, and whoever curses you I will curse; and all peoples on earth will be blessed through you." Galatians 3:8 fulfills this and talks about the promise that Jesus would come from Abraham and the nations of the world would, indeed, be blessed. It says, "And the Scripture, foreseeing that God would justify the Gentiles by faith, preached the gospel beforehand to Abraham, saying, 'In you shall all the nations be blessed.'" Galatians 3:16 solidified the fact that Jesus was a descendant of Abraham, explaining, "Now to Abraham and his seed were the promises made. He saith not, And to seeds, as of many; but as of one, And to thy seed, which is Christ." Abraham was chosen by God because of the love God had for him. The lineage would prove this point. Moses, in Gen 22:18, wrote about Abraham: "and through your offspring all nations on earth will be blessed, because you have obeyed me."

How would all nations be blessed? The savior of this world would come through Abraham's descendants. Matthew, a tax collector, explained this prophecy in the beginning of his Gospel. He was an educated man with experience in money and facts, and in chapter 1 of his book, Matthew followed the lineage of Abraham, Isaac, and Jacob, through King David and his son Solomon, all the way down to Jacob, the father of Joseph, the husband of Mary, who was the mother of Jesus, the Messiah. Matthew concluded with the following: "Thus there were fourteen generations in all from Abraham to David, fourteen from David to the exile to Babylon, and fourteen from the exile to the Messiah" (Matt 1:17). Genesis 49:10 shows us that Jesus would be the Messiah whom all nations would eventually follow as their King of kings. The author of Genesis wrote, "The scepter will not depart from Judah, nor the ruler's staff from between his feet, until he to whom it belongs shall come and the obedience of the nations shall be his" (Gen 49:10). Luke, by telling us about John the Baptist, showed how Jesus would be the one born that all people should follow. Luke said John's baptism was a sign of repentance and forgiveness of sins, and it was a way for people to commit themselves to God. John also tells people how they should behave to prepare for Jesus' arrival. In Luke 3:4–6 John the Baptist used Isaiah to tell of the coming of the ruler of the world. "As it is written in the book of the words of Isaiah the prophet: 'A voice of one calling in the wilderness, "Prepare the way for the Lord, make straight paths for him. Every valley shall be filled in, every mountain and hill made low. The crooked roads shall become straight, the rough ways smooth. And all people will see God's salvation."'"

The birth of Jesus is one of the most known stories worldwide. Luke writes about the story in chapter 2.

> In those days Caesar Augustus issued a decree that a census should be taken of the entire Roman world. (This was the first census that took place while Quirinius was governor of Syria.) And everyone went to their own town to register. So Joseph also went up from the town of Nazareth in Galilee to Judea, to Bethlehem the town

of David, because he belonged to the house and line of David. He went there to register with Mary, who was pledged to be married to him and was expecting a child. While they were there, the time came for the baby to be born, and she gave birth to her firstborn, a son. She wrapped him in cloths and placed him in a manger, because there was no guest room available for them. (Luke 1:1–7)

This, however, is not the first time the Bible tells where the Son of God would be born. In the Old Testament, Micah prophesied to the Jewish people saying, "But you, Bethlehem Ephrathah, though you are small among the clans of Judah out of you will come for me one who will be ruler over Israel" (Mic 5:2). After Jesus was born, he was presented gifts fit for a king by three magi who had been searching for the King of the Jews. "On coming to the house, they saw the child with his mother Mary, and they bowed down and worshiped him. Then they opened their treasures and presented him with gift of gold, frankincense and myrrh" (Matt 2:11). Apparently the psalmist alluded to this event when he wrote, "May the kings of Tarshish and of distant shores bring tribute to him. May the kings of Sheba and Seba present him gifts. May kings bow down to him and all nations serve him" (Ps 72:10–11).

Since the magi had told Herod of their plans to find the King of the Jews, Herod became enraged with jealousy. He ask them to tell him, when they found this baby, where he was, so he too could worship. We all know his real reason was so that he could kill this baby. No one knows the exact time that had passed after the magi had visited Jesus, but Herod sought the death of this child. Matthew wrote, "When Herod realized that he had been outwitted by the magi, he was furious, and he gave orders to kill all the boys in Bethlehem and its vicinity who were two years old and under, in accordance with the time he had learned from the magi" (Matt 2:16). Author John Calahan wrote, "King Herod the Great was wicked. So we should not be surprised that a non-Christian wrote the following about Herod's massacre of children under the age of two that is mentioned in Matt 2:16."[1] "Macrobius about the year 400, bears testimony to Herod's slaughter of the infants at Bethlehem. [He] explains to us that 'when Augustus had heard, that among the children within two years of age, which Herod king of the Jews commanded to be slain in Syria, his own son had been killed, he

---

1. Calahan, "Is There Secular Evidence."

said: "It is better to be Herod's hog than his son" (Macrobius, Saturnalia 2.f.11)."[2] "The non-Christian writer is Macrobius (AD 395–423)."[3]

The Old Testament prophecy found in Jer 31:15 seems to explain the pain the mothers would suffer in Jerusalem. The prophecy states, "This is what the Lord says: 'A voice is heard in Ramah, mourning and great weeping, Rachel weeping for her children and refusing to be comforted, because they are no more.'"

How, then, was Jesus saved from this assault on the children? The Old Testament prophecy in Hos 11:1, "Out of Egypt I called My Son," is retold in Matt 2:13: "When they had gone, an angel of the Lord appeared to Joseph in a dream. 'Get up,' he said, 'take the child and his mother and escape to Egypt. Stay there until I tell you, for Herod is going to search for the child to kill him.'"

Even though the messages and prophecies found in the Old Testament do not always match word for word, 100 percent, to the New Testament passages, they often infer the meaning God has as he talks through his prophets like Hosea, David, Isaiah, and Jeremiah. The prophets of old told many messages from God, himself, to the people of Israel. Many of them predicted God would send them light and joy through the birth of a child who would break the "yoke of [their] burden" (Isa 9:4). He also said, "For unto us a child is born, unto us a son is given; and the government shall be upon his shoulder: and his name shall be called Wonderful, Counselor, Mighty God, Everlasting Father, Prince of Peace" (Isa 9:6). The followers of Jesus also call him the Son of God and Abba Father. Jesus was, indeed, their counselor. Jesus even described the Holy Spirit as another counselor, or "advocate" in John 14:16. In other words, Jesus saying that he himself had been a counselor to his disciples when he was with them here on this earth.

The Old Testament truly prophesied the man Jesus and how he was born and what happened to him as a child. But the prophecies go far beyond that. They also foretold the nature of Jesus. The Messiah possessed the attributes of God. They were, and we are, saying that Jesus was actually God. I have said that he is the "I Am." In John 8:58, Jesus, himself, makes this claim. We will delve further into the prophecies concerning his nature in the next chapter.

---

2. Smollett, "Macrobius and the Slaughter of the Innocents."

3. Calahan, "Is There Secular Evidence."

Chapter 4

PROPHECIES OF THE NATURE OF JESUS

To BEGIN LOOKING AT THE NATURE of Jesus, it is probably important to understand that the man claiming to be the Messiah was, undoubtedly, a real person. Yes, many people believe, but is there actual evidence of his existence? To establish facts of the existence of something, science must use indisputable observation. To prove the same about the existence of a person, however, a provable source from another person or persons is needed. In the case of Jesus there are many independent sources There are twelve sources we know about who knew and followed Jesus as disciples. But, there are also people who did not follow Jesus yet wrote about his existence in the first century. The most famous are probably Tacitus, a Roman historian who mentioned Jesus in his writings called *The Histories and the Annals*, and Yosef ben Mattityahu, who was a Roman–Jewish historian and military leader, better known as Flavius Josephus.

Tacitus is a main source in understanding Roman life and history. He wrote about the empire of Rome from AD 14 to AD 68. In his *Histories* he explained how the emperor, Nero, placed blame for most of the ills facing Rome on a band of Jews who were hated by the people. These Jewish men and women, and some Greeks and Romans, were called Christians because they followed a man named Jesus, the Christ. Tacitus wrote:

> Christus, from whom the name had its origin, suffered the extreme penalty during the reign of Tiberius at the hands of one of our procurators, Pontius Pilatus, and a most mischievous superstition, thus checked for the moment, again broke out not only in Judea, the first source of the evil, but even in Rome, where all

things hideous and shameful from every part of the world find their center and become popular.[1]

The hatred of the Christians and their leader was countered by another writer. Flavius Josephus also wrote about the Christ, but in a positive light. He explained:

> Now, there was about this time Jesus, a wise man, if it be lawful to call him a man, for he was a doer of wonderful works—a teacher of such men as receive the truth with pleasure. He drew over to him both many of the Jews, and many of the Gentiles. He was the Christ, and when Pilate, at the suggestion of the principal men among us, had condemned him to the cross, those that loved him at the first did not forsake him; for he appeared to them alive again the third day; as the divine prophets had foretold these and ten thousand other wonderful things concerning him. And the tribe of Christians so named from him are not extinct at this day.[2]

Jesus, then, was a living man. He, however, possesses the nature of God, because he is God. Micah 5:2, in the Old Testament, says, "But you, O Bethlehem Ephrathah, though you be little among the thousands of Judah, yet out of thee shall he come forth unto me that is to be ruler in Israel; whose goings forth have been from of old, from everlasting." This prophet was declaring that the child that would eventually be born in Bethlehem would be God in the flesh.

John 17:1–5 fulfilled this when Jesus was praying to his Father in heaven.

> After Jesus said this, he looked toward heaven and prayed: "Father, the hour has come. Glorify your Son, that your Son may glorify you. For you granted him authority over all people that he might give eternal life to all those you have given him. Now this is eternal life: that they know you, the only true God, and Jesus Christ, whom you have sent. I have brought you glory on earth by finishing the work you gave me to do. And now, Father, glorify me in your presence with the glory I had with you before the world began."

Micah used the words "from everlasting," and Jesus confessed that he had been with God since before the world began.

Another fulfillment of Micah's is found in Col 1:15–17.

---

1. Kirby, "Cornelius Tacitus," quoting from *Annals* 15.44.
2. Josephus, *Antiquities of the Jews* 18.63.

> For in him all things were created: things in heaven and on earth, visible and invisible, whether thrones or powers or rulers or authorities; all things have been created through him and for him. He is before all things, and in him all things hold together. And he is the head of the body, the church; he is the beginning and the firstborn from among the dead, so that in everything he might have the supremacy. For God was pleased to have all his fullness dwell in him, and through him to reconcile to himself all things, whether things on earth or things in heaven, by making peace through his blood, shed on the cross.

God's fullness was found in Jesus, and he was, indeed, God.

The disciple John explained this in the words that Jesus spoke. In John 8:58, Jesus says, "Before Abraham was, I am." Jesus said "I am" many times, but this one expressed that he was the Son of God, but also God. The term he used was the same title that God used in Exod 3:13–14 to explain who he was. Moses said to God, "Suppose I go to the Israelites and say to them, 'The God of your fathers has sent me to you,' and they ask me, 'What is his name?' Then what shall I tell them?"—God said to Moses, "I am who I am. This is what you are to say to the Israelites: 'I am has sent me to you.'"

Jesus, the I AM, was at the beginning of all things, but he would also be a mediator between God and man. Job, in the Old Testament, wished that he could have a mediator between himself and God, but realized he could not argue with God because God was not mortal. Job said, "For He is not a man, as I am, that I may answer Him, and that we should go to court together. Nor is there any mediator between us, who may lay his hand on us both" (Job 9:32–33). Job wished for someone who could be a negotiator. The words were fulfilled when Jesus came. First Timothy 2:5–6 was written to assure us. "For there is one God and one mediator between God and mankind, the man Christ Jesus, who gave himself as a ransom for all people. This has now been witnessed to at the proper time."

The nature of Jesus was to be God and to be a mediator between God and man. He was holy, merciful, and the spiritual rock of Israel. Moses is credited with writing the song in Exod 15. Chapter 15:2 states, "The Lord is my strength and my defense; he has become my salvation. He is my God, and I will praise him, my father's God, and I will exalt him." Yeshua, the Messiah, was written about in Acts 7:55–56: "But Stephen, full of the Holy Spirit, looked up to heaven and saw the glory of God, and Jesus standing at the right hand of God. 'Look,' he said, 'I see heaven open and the Son of Man standing at the right hand of God.'" So, Jesus (Yeshua) was holy. We could question his nature, as in Exod 15:11, "Who among the gods is like you, Lord? Who is like you—majestic in holiness, awesome in glory, working wonders?" Or we could say what John was told to write in Rev 3:7. "To the angel of the church in Philadelphia write: These are the words of him who is holy and true, who holds the key of David. What he opens no one can shut, and what he shuts no one can open." The holy and true one, who has the power of God because he is God, is also the spiritual rock of Israel. Moses, in Exod 17:6, struck a rock and God provided life-giving water to the people of Israel. Paul, in 1 Cor 10:4, is alluding to Moses and the life-giving water that came from the rock, and is making a spiritual comparison to those among Israel in his day. He wrote, "They all ate the same spiritual food and drank the same spiritual drink; for they drank from the spiritual rock that accompanied them, and that rock was Christ." The Christ, which is from the Greek word *christos* and the Hebrew word *mashiach*, means "anointed one": God in the flesh.

How can Jesus, though, make this claim? He said, "I and the Father are one" (John 10:30). The Bible speaks of God as the Father of us all in the book of Philippians. Titus states that God is the Son, and in Acts 5:3–4 God is presented as the Holy Spirit. All three are God. How is that possible?

I found the answer in my own writings. I have written many times concerning the belief of the Trinity. God is actually three in one. He is the Father, the Son, and the Holy Spirit. To understand that, look at yourself. You are also three in one because mankind is tripartite. You have a body. It is the flesh and blood that is inhabited by your spirit and your soul: body, spirit, and soul, or three in one. One day, our spirit and soul will leave our body, and how you have chosen to live will determine where you go.

The soul is your intellect, your emotions, and your will. We know right from wrong. We know we have free will. Sometimes, we let our emotions control what we do, and even if we know it may be wrong, we try to justify what we have done. It is then the spirit might condemn us for what we have done, because the spirit is our conscience. It makes us feel guilty. Because the soul knows right from wrong, and we choose wrong, the spirit steps in and makes us feel guilty.

Therefore, we have a body, a soul, and a spirit. God, too, is a soul. He is a personage, in that he is a being who possesses a mind, emotion, and will. He creates, he loves, and he feels emotion. God is a Spirit. The Holy Spirit condemns us when we commit sin. God is also a body. His body was sent to this earth as the Messiah, who would live and die and rise again, to show us we could live, die, and have eternal life.

In Gen 1:26 God creates humans in his image. He says, "Let us make mankind in our image, in our likeness, so that they may rule over the fish in the sea and the birds in the sky, over the livestock and all the wild animals, and over all the creatures that move along the ground." The words "let us" include the three in one, the Father, the Son, and the Holy Spirit. All three parts of our God existed before everything. The Old Testament stated this and the New Testament proved it.

Because of this, it is easier to understand why we call Jesus our Lord. The prophecy in Ps 110:1 tells us, "The LORD said unto my Lord, Sit thou at my right hand, until I make thine enemies thy footstool." This song writer, King David, is explaining that Christ will be seated at the right hand of God. He will be waiting for the appointed time when God gives him the word and he will return to earth to defeat his enemies, Satan, his fallen angels, and the demons who serve him. Matthew 22:43–45 fulfills the Psalms when Jesus was talking to the Pharisees about who the Messiah would be. They answered that he would be the son of David. When Jesus used Ps 110, he asked the Pharisees why King David calls the Christ "my Lord" if the Christ is his son. This raises the issue of how Christ is divine and totally baffles the Pharisees.

That brings us to the prophecy that Jesus would be called Immanuel. The name Immanuel is from the Hebrew name לְאוּנְּמָע ('Emmanuel) meaning "God is with us," from the roots עִם ('im) meaning "with" and לְא ('el) meaning "God," and Isa 7:14 states, "Therefore the Lord himself will give you a sign: the virgin will conceive and give birth to a son, and will call him Emmanuel." Matthew 1:23 fulfills the words of Isiah saying, "Behold, a virgin shall be with child, and shall bring forth a son, And they shall call his name Emmanuel, which being interpreted is, God with us." He was sent by God, as God, that people might have eternal life. God will glorify the Son and the Son will glorify the Father. As stated before, Moses prophesied this exclaiming the coming of the final King of Israel, the Messiah himself.

In the fifth book of the Old Testament, Deuteronomy, the author foretells that this Messiah would be a prophet. In Deut 18:18, Moses wrote, "I will raise up for them a prophet like you from among their kindred, and will put my words into the mouth of the prophet; the prophet shall tell them all that I command. Anyone who will not listen to my words which the prophet speaks in my name, I myself will hold accountable for it." In the New Testament, Matthew explained how the crowds described Jesus. He said, "The crowds answered, 'This is Jesus, the prophet from Nazareth in Galilee.'" Matthew 21:11 is the crucial verse that shows us that Jesus was a prophet from Nazareth during his triumphant entry into Jerusalem. The people first recognized him as a prophet who fulfilled the words written by Moses. The crowd, however turned on Jesus a week later, showing the inconsistency of mankind's empathy and loyalties. According to Moses, though, these people would be held accountable for what they have done.

Not only does the Old Testament describe the Messiah as a prophet, it also states that he will be a priest. In Ps 110:4 David, who composed many of the songs found there, wrote, "The Lord hath sworn, and will not repent, Thou art a priest for ever after the order of Melchizedek." Melchizedek, in the Bible, was the king of Salem and high priest of El Elyon. He was first mentioned in Gen 14:18–20, where he brought out bread and wine and then blessed Abram and El Elyon, which is another name that appears in the Hebrew Bible and in English means "God Most High." Isaiah 33:22 reads, "For the Lord is our judge, the Lord is our lawgiver, the LORD is our king; it is he who will save us." The lawgivers of old were the priests of the Jews. That is why it is reported by Paul the apostle, in Heb 3:1, "Therefore, holy brothers, who share in the heavenly calling, fix your thoughts on Jesus, the apostle and high priest whom we confess. He was faithful to the one who appointed him, just as Moses was faithful in all God's house." Jesus was the High Priest who answered only to God.

Like the priest Melchizedek, king of Salem, Jesus too was prophesied as a king. In Ps 2:6 David sings to the Lord, "I have installed my king on Zion, my holy mountain." This passage predicts the anointed King—the Messiah—will eventually rule all kingdoms, and the psalmist urges the kings and rulers of the earth to submit to the Son's rule. In Matt 27:37, the disciple explains how the Romans placed a sign on the cross. He wrote, "And over his head they put the charge against him, which read, 'This is Jesus, the King of the Jews.'" This sign explains how another prophecy was fulfilled by the Christ.

Jesus was the Christ. "Christ" is not a name, it is a title. It means "Messiah, Anointed One, or Chosen One." Isaiah was the prophet who prophesied that about the Messiah, saying in Isa 11:2, "The Spirit of the LORD shall rest upon Him, the Spirit of wisdom and understanding, the Spirit of counsel and might, the Spirit of knowledge and of the fear of the LORD." He was stating that the Spirit of God would rest on a descendant of Jesse, the father of King David. The Lord's Spirit, as explained by Isaiah, was the Spirit of wisdom and understanding. This means that this future leader would rule with these qualities as well as the spirit of counsel and might. The fulfillment of this prophetic verse was found when Matthew wrote, "As soon as Jesus was baptized, he went up out of the water. At that moment heaven was opened, and he saw the Spirit of God descending like a dove and alighting on him. And a voice from heaven said, 'This is my Son, whom I love; with him I am well pleased'" (Matt 3:16–17).

Finally, writing of the nature of Jesus, it must be said that the Messiah must possess an unquenching zeal for God. Zeal, as defined in dictionary terms, is the excessive fervor to do something or accomplish some end. Psalm 69:9 says, "For zeal for your house consumes me, and the insults of those who insult you fall on me." In other words, this psalm and this very emotional verse explain the psalmist's deep love and devotion to God, the pain he feels about those who dishonor God's house, and the willingness to suffer whatever happens because of that love. It makes sense, then, to compare this as a prophecy describing Jesus. We all know the story that John shared when Jesus went to the temple and saw the money changers. John 2:14–18 shows the zeal, and even anger, Jesus displayed at that moment. "In the temple courts he found people selling cattle, sheep and doves, and others sitting at tables exchanging money. So he made a whip out of cords, and drove all from the temple courts, both sheep and cattle; he scattered the coins of the money changers and overturned their tables. To those who sold doves he said, 'Get these out of here! Stop turning my Father's house into a market!'" His disciples remembered that it is written: "Zeal for your house will consume me."

I started out by saying that Jesus was real, and he possesses the nature of God. God is spirit. He is transcendent and doesn't follow physical laws. He is eternal and all powerful. He is all loving and all knowing. Jesus possessed the attributes and nature of God because he was the Son of God and, indeed, God. He showed this at birth, as an adult preaching to the people, as a Savior hanging on the cross, and as a risen Lord who defeated death.

Chapter 5

PROPHESIED LIFE OF
THE SON OF GOD

The Old Testament has told us that Jesus would be born, live among his people, and die for us. We also have been told that he would rise again and defeat death. He would ascend to the Father in heaven and, contrary to popular belief, he would come again to defeat Satan once and for all. What proof, however, exists? The nature of Christ is the nature of God, but Jesus came to earth as a human, too. He was to fulfill the Old Testament's prophecy concerning the man who would be the King and the Messiah.

When, then, was the "Anointed One" ("messiah" in Hebrew) to be born? In Dan 9, it was predicted that the Messiah would be born before the destruction of the Second Temple found on the Temple Mount in Jerusalem. Around AD 70, during the Jewish–Roman War, the Romans destroyed the temple, except for a piece of the western wall, which can be seen to this day.

In Dan 9:24–26 it was written that the Messiah would be born and that it would happen before the destruction of the temple by Rome. Daniel said,

> Seventy "sevens" are decreed for your people and your holy city to finish transgression, to put an end to sin, to atone for wickedness, to bring in everlasting righteousness, to seal up vision and prophecy and to anoint the Most Holy Place. Know and understand this: From the time the word goes out to restore and rebuild Jerusalem until the Anointed One, the ruler, comes there will be seven "sevens," and sixty-two "sevens." It will be rebuilt with streets

and a trench, but in times of trouble. After the sixty-two "sevens," the Anointed One will be put to death and will have nothing. The people of the ruler who will come will destroy the city and the sanctuary.

Daniel's prayer to God requests that he will intercede on behalf of the Jewish people and the Jewish city, Jerusalem. He received an answer from the angel Gabriel. The angel prophesied that seventy "weeks" were appointed for Daniel's people and the city of Jerusalem. The prophecy included the coming of a messiah and also a time of distress for Israel. The temple would be destroyed after Jesus had come, lived, and died.

Daniel was not the only prophet to tell of the coming Messiah. Abraham, a servant of the Lord, also received a promise from God. Abraham was born under the name Abram in Babylonia He was alive about 1,800 years before the birth of the Christ Child. During that time, God promised Abraham the entire world would be blessed through his descendants It would be from Abraham that the Messiah would be born. Genesis 12:3 tells us about the beginning of God's relationship with Abram and the first step in building God's people Israel. God made a covenant with Abram, also known as Abraham, that he would "bless those who bless you, and the one who curses you I will curse. And in you all the families of the earth will be blessed." Matthew 1:1 starts out by saying, "The genealogy of Jesus Christ, the Son of David, the Son of Abraham . . . ." The descendants of Abraham would lead to the Messiah. Acts 3:25–26 explained, "You are sons of the prophets, and of the covenant which God made with our fathers, saying to Abraham, 'And in your seed all the families of the earth shall be blessed.' To you first, God, having raised up His Servant Jesus, sent Him to bless you, in turning away every one of you from your iniquities." In this passage, Peter was preaching at the temple gate and explaining how Jesus suffered. He stated that the people acted foolishly but that their foolishness fulfilled God's prophecy. He said that the crowd gathered there needed to repent, and he warned them what would happen if they kept rejecting Jesus.

One of the descendants of Abraham was David. With his words, David prophesied, in a roundabout way, that Jesus came to do God's will. David, the author of many psalms, stated, "Here I am, I have come—it is written about me in the scroll. I desire to do your will, my God; your law is within my heart" (Ps 40:7–8). Matthew 26:39 fulfills this psalm's words when Jesus was praying to his Father in heaven. Matthew writes, "He went a little farther and fell on His face, and prayed, saying, 'O My Father, if it is possible, let this cup pass from Me; nevertheless, not as I will, but as You will.'" Paul wrote the words that Jesus spoke in his letter to the Hebrews. He reported the words Jesus stated were "Here I am—it is written about me in the scroll—I have come to do your will, my God" (Heb 10:9).

Jesus was born, then, for this purpose. He was fulfilling the will of God. That is the reason he was, as we discussed earlier, born of a virgin in Bethlehem, worshiped by the shepherds, visited by the magi, and taken to Egypt to be protected from Herod. When he was ready for his ministry, he was preceded by a messenger who was preparing the way for him. He spread his message all over and taught all that we should love God and love others as we love ourselves. He came to earth not as a king but as a servant. He didn't come for the rich and famous; he came for the needy and weak. "For he will deliver the needy who cry out, the afflicted who have no one to help. He will take pity on the weak and the needy and save the needy from death. He will rescue them from oppression and violence, for precious is their blood in his sight" (Ps 72:12–14). This psalm is describing and predicting why the Messiah would come. John the Baptist heard of the things Jesus was doing. He sent two of his men to ask Jesus if he was the one who was to come. In Luke 7:22 he told us, "So He [Jesus] replied to the messengers, 'Go back and report to John what you have seen and heard: The blind receive sight, the lame walk, those who have leprosy are cleansed, the deaf hear, the dead are raised, and the good news is proclaimed to the poor.'"

When the prophet Isaiah spoke, it was indeed a message from God. He explained to the people of Israel the coming of the Messiah many times. On one occasion he said, "Here is my servant, whom I uphold, my chosen one in whom I delight; I will put my Spirit on him, and he will bring justice to the nations." In Matt 12, Jesus is healing the sick and downtrodden on the Sabbath. The Pharisees, seeing this, wanted Jesus gone. Jesus knew the Pharisees were out to kill him, so he withdrew from the area and another crowd gathered. Jesus healed the hand of a disfigured man there and told the crowd not to tell others what they had seen. He said, "This was to fulfill what was spoken through the prophet Isaiah: Here is my servant whom I have chosen, the one I love, in whom I delight; I will put my Spirit on him, and he will proclaim justice to the nations."

Jesus was pleasing to his Father and was on earth to do God's will. He was blessed with the Holy Spirit and was very much like the tabernacle where God dwelt among the Israelites. Actually, the word "tabernacle" means "dwelling place." It was a sanctuary where the people could go and be close to God. He was there so his people could worship him and he could be with them. Jesus, as the tabernacle, could be the fulfilled connection between God and man.

Isaiah 7:14 foreshadowed the birth of the Messiah when Isaiah said, "Therefore the Lord himself will give you a sign: The virgin will conceive and give birth to a son, and will call him Immanuel." The name Immanuel, as we have defined before, means "God with us," and John, the apostle, in John 1:14 defined Jesus as "the Word became flesh and made his dwelling among us. We have seen his glory, the glory of the one and only Son, who came from the Father, full of grace and truth." John said that Jesus was the tangible evidence that God was with us, and Matthew even took it further. Matthew 1:21–23 shows us that she (Mary) "'will give birth to a son, and you are to give him the name Jesus, because he will save his people from their sins.' All this took place to fulfill what the Lord had said through the prophet: 'The virgin will conceive and give birth to a son, and they will call him Immanuel.'" We know that this means "God with us," so Jesus fulfilled another biblical verse as the promised one who would be the deliverer of the Jewish nation prophesied in the Hebrew Bible.

As "Jesus grew in wisdom and in favor of God and man," as Luke wrote (2:52), he also showed other attributes of fulfilling prophecy. Jesus would perform miracles to show that he was "God with us." In Isa 29:18, the prophet declared, "In that day the deaf will hear the words of the scroll, and out of gloom and darkness the eyes of the blind will see." Isaiah may have been showing the spiritual deafness and blindness of the Israelites, but he was also outlining the miracles Jesus would perform. The Messiah helped the blind see. Matthew 9:27–29 explains how Jesus healed two blind men. "As Jesus went on from there, two blind men followed him, calling out, 'Have mercy on us, Son of David!' When he had gone indoors, the blind men came to him, and he asked them, 'Do you believe that I am able to do this?' 'Yes, Lord,' they replied. Then he touched their eyes and said, 'According to your faith let it be done to you'; and their sight was restored."

As Isaiah foretold, Jesus would help the deaf hear. In Mark 7:32–35 it was written, "They brought to him a man who was deaf and had a speech impediment, and they begged him to lay his hand on him. And taking him aside from the crowd privately, he put his fingers into his ears, and after spitting touched his tongue. And looking up to heaven, he sighed and said to him, 'Ephphatha,' that is, 'Be opened.' And his ears were opened, his tongue was released, and he spoke plainly."

Jesus would not only cause the blind to see and the mute to talk, he would also command that the lame would walk. Hundreds of years before the Christ, in Isa 35:5–6, this man who spoke the words of God would speak of the day of the Messiah this way: "Then the eyes of the blind shall be opened, and the ears of the deaf unstopped; then shall the lame man leap like a deer, and the tongue of the mute sing for Joy." Isaiah's prophecies came true as Jesus performed what only the Son of God could do.

Jesus was the healer, but he said he was also the living water. We all know that without water, we would die. Living water is a metaphor explaining that without Jesus we would not have the life-giving properties of water. We could not be refreshed and live without Jesus. Living water was given to the people of Israel as described in Exod 17:6. When the Israelite were in the desert and there was no water for them to drink. Therefore, God spoke to Moses, "I will stand there before you by the rock at Horeb. Strike the rock, and water will come out of it for the people to drink." So Moses did this in the sight of the elders of Israel. Once again, fulfillment was realized while Jesus was in Samaria.

When a Samaritan women came to the well where Jesus was, he asked her for a drink. Because Jews did not associate with Samaritan, the woman was surprised. She answered, "You are a Jew and I am a Samaritan woman. How can you ask me for a drink?" Jesus answered her, "If you knew the gift of God and who it is that asks you for a drink, you would have asked him and he would have given you living water" (John 4:10). Jesus was like the living water, but in the Old Testament he was compared and contrasted to Adam and Moses. First, in comparing and contrasting Jesus to Adam, we look to Gen 2:17. Adam sinned against God and, because he was disobedient, God said, "Thou shalt surely die." Because of Adam's sin, all mankind would die. On the other hand, Jesus was sinless, and Christ's obedience is greater than Adam's disobedience. In other words, the rightness of Jesus is given to followers when they decide to accept him as their Lord and Savior. Jesus was known as the new Adam. Because Adam was the first head of all earthly families, Jesus was the new Adam, the head of the spiritual family. Romans 5:15 emphasizes this when the author writes, "The many died by the trespass of the one man, how much more did God's grace and the gift that came by the grace of the one man, Jesus Christ, overflow to the many!"

Like Adam, Moses was also compared and contrasted to Jesus. Moses, himself, told the people that there would be another prophet just like him. In Deut 18:15, he said, "The Lord your God will raise up for you a prophet like me from among you, from your fellow Israelites. You must listen to him." Moses led his people from the slavery of Egypt and showed them freedom. God chose Moses and told him, "I will be with you, and when you bring the people out of Egypt, you will worship me on this mountain. That will be the proof that I have sent you" (Exod 3:12). It was as if God, himself, had come to save his children. In Luke 19:10, the story of God saving the Israelites is retold when it is explained "for the Son of Man came to seek and to save the lost." Jesus, too, came to save his people. Because of this, he has given us all a choice of living in sin or finding the freedom from sin through him.

Jesus came to save, and he did so even when someone had died. In Luke 7:16, another prophecy was realized. The story concerns itself with a time when Jesus "approached the town gate, and a dead person was being carried out—the only son of his mother, and she was a widow. And a large crowd from the town was with her. When the Lord saw her, his heart went out to her and he said, 'Don't cry.' Then he went up and touched the bier they were carrying him on, and the bearers stood still. He said, 'Young man, I say to you, get up!' The dead man sat up and began to talk, and Jesus gave him back to his mother. They were all filled with awe and praised God. 'A great prophet has appeared among us,' they said. 'God has come to help his people.'" The words of the Old Testament are truly repeated in this man named Jesus.

Although the Old Testament did not specifically foretell of the Messiah resurrecting the dead, it was widely accepted, in Gen 22, that Abraham believed God would bring Isaac back from the dead if he obeyed the Lord and used his son as a sacrifice. To Abraham, it would be an act of obedience and worship. He trusted God perfectly even in the event that his son would die.

Hebrews 11:19 explained how Abraham felt when he was about to sacrifice his only son, as God had ordered. Paul wrote, "By faith Abraham, when he was tried, offered up Isaac: and he that had received the promises offered up his only begotten son, Of whom it was said, that in Isaac shall thy seed be called: Accounting that God was able to raise him up, even from the dead; from whence also he received him in a figurative sense."

Jesus, then, because of all he did and showed, was the Old Testament's words fulfilled. In Deuteronomy, Moses told the people that God's laws were not unattainable. Moses explained that they may never be perfect, but they did have a choice. They could give their hearts to God, thereby choosing life over death. They must keep the word of God in their hearts and mouths. Moses wrote, "The word is very near you; it is in your mouth and in your heart so you may obey it." Jesus, too, is the Word. In John 1:1, the disciple remarked, "In the beginning was the Word, and the Word was with God, and the Word was God." Jesus was in the hearts of his followers, too. What is really being stated here, by his disciples, is that Jesus was not only the Son of God, he was God. Even so, his family rejected that their brother could be the one sent by God. This was first recorded in the prophetic message written by the psalmist in Ps 69:8, which says, "I am a foreigner to my own family, a stranger to my own mother's children." Just like this writer of songs, Jesus faced the same problem. In fulfilling this prophecy, Jesus went with his disciples to dine with them. "Jesus entered a house, and again a crowd gathered, so that he and his disciples were not even able to eat. When his family heard about this, they went to take charge of him, for they said, 'He is out of his mind'" (Mark 3:20, 21). The brothers of Jesus did not understand the nature of the Christ, or maybe they were afraid of him. They turned on him, and in John 7:3–5, they turned on him and told him to leave Galilee. In a way, this is why the people, too, turned on Jesus and started to plot against him. He was a danger to those in power because he was described as the one who came in the name of the Lord.

Before his capture, Jesus ate a last supper with his disciples. This last supper may have been foreshadowed in the time of Abraham. In Gen 14:18 the author tells of a meeting between Abraham and two kings, one who was named Melchizedek. This is the first time that a king was introduced as a priest, a genuine priest of God. Melchizedek was a man from Canaan who served the God of Israel. This was even before Israel existed and before Yahweh (God) was known by that name. It was written, "Then Melchizedek, king of Salem, brought out bread and wine. He was priest of God Most High." Matthew tells of what became the well-known rite of communion. "While they were eating, Jesus took bread, and when he had given thanks, he broke it and gave it to his disciples, saying, 'Take and eat; this is my body.' Then he took a cup, and when he had given thanks, he gave it to them, saying, 'Drink from it, all of you. This is my blood of the covenant, which is poured out for many for the forgiveness of sins. I tell you, I will not drink from this fruit of the vine from now on until that day when I drink it new with you in my Father's kingdom'" (Matt 26:26–29).

It was after the Last Supper that the plot to arrest Jesus began. The Psalms foretold this. Psalm 2:1, 2 questioned, "Why do the nations conspire and the peoples plot in vain? The kings of the earth rise up and the rulers band together against the Lord and against his anointed." In Matt 12:14, the author simply wrote, "But the Pharisees went out and plotted how they might kill Jesus." Luke furthered this by writing, "Then the whole assembly rose and led him off to Pilate" (Luke 23:1).

We have all told the story of how they captured Jesus and about his betrayer's kiss. Jesus had been betrayed by one of his own, and that was why they captured him. Once again, it was the psalmist who foretold this in Ps 41:9. He wrote, "Even my close friend, someone I trusted, one who shared my bread, has turned against me." How precise the prophesies of the Old Testament were. The New Testament tells the story of Judas, one of the Twelve who broke bread with the Savior. Mark 14:10–11 explained almost word for word the prophecy told in Psalms. Mark wrote, "Then Judas Iscariot, one of the Twelve, went to the chief priests to betray Jesus to them. They were delighted to hear this and promised to give him money. So he watched for an opportunity to hand him over."

Judas was given money for his act of betrayal. Matthew 26:15 showed us what Judas asked, "'What are you willing to give me if I deliver him over to you?' So they counted out for him thirty pieces of silver." The Old Testament book of Zech 11:13 mirrors this bargain: In this passage, Zechariah asks the priests to pay him what he is worth, and they give him thirty pieces of silver.

Judas, after realizing what he had done, returned the money and went out and hanged himself. Matthew 27:6 explains what the chief priests did. "The chief priests picked up the coins and said, 'It is against the law to put this into the treasury, since it is blood money.' So they decided to use the money to buy the potter's field as a burial place for [the poor and] foreigners." It is getting less and less surprising to find an Old Testament verse that seems to prophetically explain the New Testament. Zechariah's words do exactly this. Zechariah, in 11:12–13, after a payment was due, said, "'If you think it best, give me my pay; but if not, keep it.' So they paid me thirty pieces of silver. And the Lord said to me, 'Throw it to the potter'—the handsome price at which they valued me! So I took the thirty pieces of silver and threw them to the potter at the house of the Lord."

After the betrayal and when Jesus had been captured, he was asked many questions. Those who sought to kill him wanted to trick him into admitting he had committed blasphemy, but he remained silent. This happened in the Old Testament and was recorded in the Psalms. David wrote,

"My God, whom I praise, do not remain silent, for people who are wicked and deceitful have opened their mouths against me; they have spoken against me with lying tongues. With words of hatred they surround me; they attack me without cause. In return for my friendship they accuse me, but I am a man of prayer. They repay me evil for good, and hatred for my friendship" (Ps 109:1–5). At they point, David refrained from responding, leaving everything in the hands of God. Jesus, too, remained silent among his accusers. Matthew wrote in Matt 26:62–63: During his trial at the palace of the Jewish high priest, Caiaphas, the high priest asked Jesus, "Answer thou nothing? What is it which these witness against thee?" but Jesus remained silent. Jesus, however, forgave his enemies. In Luke 23:34, Jesus forgave by saying, "Father, forgive them, for they do not know what they do." This, of course, was said on the cross, which leads us to the Old Testament prophecies concerning the death of the Son of God. In the New Testament, the fulfillment of those prophecies is evidenced. Isaiah, in 53:5, exclaimed, "But he was pierced for our transgressions, he was crushed for our iniquities; the punishment that brought us peace was on him, and by his wounds we are healed." In 1 Pet 2:24–25, the author explained Isaiah's words. "He himself bore our sins in his body on the cross, so that we might die to sins and live for righteousness; by his wounds you have been healed. For you were like sheep going astray, but now you have returned to the Shepherd and Overseer of your souls."

Chapter 6

PROPHESIED DEATH
OF A SON

JESUS WAS CRUCIFIED AROUND thirty-three years after his birth. His death was by a decree from Pontius Pilate after he was arrested by the Sanhedrin, the judicial body that served as the court of Jewish law. The Sanhedrin held a trial filled with false accusations and found Jesus guilty of blasphemy. Because Jews, under Roman law, could not sentence people to death, they presented their case to the Roman governor, Pontius Pilate. Pilate convened his own trial but could find no wrong in this man. He had Jesus beaten and sent to Herod, who ridiculed Jesus and then sent him back to Pilate because he was afraid of the political trouble that might arise. Pilate told the crowd that it was tradition to release one prisoner in honor of the Passover festival, and the crowd shouted that they wanted Jesus crucified. Pilate gave in to their demands and sentenced an innocent man to his death. Before the crucifixion took place, Pilate had Jesus scourged. A scourge consisted of a rope with bones or spikes at the end, used to tear the flesh of the victim.

There were forms of crucifixion earlier than the Romans, but under Roman rule they had been perfected. Crucifixions probably began with the Assyrians or Babylonians and also were practiced by the Persians. As far back as the sixth century BC, stakes and trees, not crosses, were used to end the life of prisoners. Before that, many people were hung in this way, but it was usually after they were already dead by other methods. Crucifixions were a method of Roman death for five hundred years, until Constantine I abolished it in the fourth century AD.

The crucifixion of the Christ, then, happened at a time long after the Old Testament prophecies had been written. Isaiah prophesied the crucifixion seven hundred years before Jesus was even born. The Psalms were prophetic in describing in detail how the Messiah would die for the salvation of God's people, although the Psalms were written by different authors, including Moses; Asaph, who was a singer and prophet in the court of King David; the sons of Korah, who are also known to have written psalms, as did Solomon and David. The prophecies of the crucifixions found in the Psalms, then, were written anywhere from 1500 BC to 450 BC. It is amazing how the prophets told of the death of the Son of God, the Messiah, before crucifixion was even invented.

What exactly, though, were the prophetic messages given by God to the prophets of old? Exodus 12, for example, discusses the Passover in Egypt during the time of Moses. Each Jewish family was to sacrifice a lamb and spread the blood on the mantel and door-frames so that death would pass over that house, thereby saving the people of God. In John 1:29–36 the disciple explains the prophecy and tells of John the Baptist. He wrote:

> The next day John saw Jesus coming toward him and said, "Look, the Lamb of God, who takes away the sin of the world! This is the one I meant when I said, A man who comes after me has surpassed me because he was before me. I myself did not know him, but the reason I came baptizing with water was that he might be revealed to Israel." Then John gave this testimony: "I saw the Spirit come down from heaven as a dove and remain on him. And I myself did not know him, but the one who sent me to baptize with water told me, The man on whom you see the Spirit come down and remain is the one who will baptize with the Holy Spirit. I have seen and I testify that this is God's Chosen One."

This chosen one was the Son of God who would die to save mankind from eternal separation from God after death. In doing so, he would defeat Satan and death itself. Moses wrote, in Deut 32:43, that "God will avenge the blood of his servants and render vengeance to his adversaries." It is the affirmation of God's justice. God would not allow for the persecution of his children to go unpunished. In Heb 2:17, Paul talks about how the prophecy of Moses was answered: "Therefore he had to be made like his brothers in every respect, so that he might become a merciful and faithful high priest in the service of God, to make propitiation for the sins of the people." Moses promised God would atone for his people. Jesus' sacrifice is that atonement.

Christ was God who became a man, in order to completely vanquish the devil's power of sin and death over mankind.

There are certainly more prophetic passages in the Old Testament that were completed because of Jesus. The author of Ps 38:11 will not be shaken because the will of God is what must happen. God will be in control even when the foundation of your faith is tested, even when the world is against you, and even if everyone abandons you. This psalmist wrote that his friends would abandon him when he remarked, "My loved ones and friends stand back from my affliction, and my relatives stand at a distance." Whatever his affliction was or whatever he was going through, his friends abandoned him and his family was not standing by him. Jesus was arrested by the Jewish leaders and during that night all of his friends fled in fear. Matthew 26:56–58 tells us, "But this has all taken place that the writings of the prophets might be fulfilled. Then all the disciples deserted him and fled," and Mark (14:50) simply stated, "Then everyone deserted him and fled."

Jesus stood before his accusers with no one left to defend him. His trial was a sham. The Gospel of Mark shows that "the chief priests and the whole Sanhedrin were looking for evidence against Jesus so that they could put him to death, but they did not find any. Many testified falsely against him, but their statements did not agree. Then some stood up and gave this false testimony against him: We heard him say, 'I will destroy this temple made with human hands and in three days will build another, not made with hands.' Yet even then their testimony did not agree." False accusations are found in Ps 27:12, which reads, "Do not turn me over to the desire of my foes, for false witnesses rise up against me, spouting malicious accusations." David is asking God for deliverance, but even if he faces falsehoods, it is God's will and help that we must follow.

One of the closest and, by the way, my favorite prophetic comparisons is found when Isaiah wrote of the coming Messiah, saying, "I offered my back to those who beat me, my cheeks to those who pulled out my beard; I did not hide my face from mocking and spitting" (Isa 50:6). He wrote about the abuse the Messiah would receive at the hands of the Romans and the Jewish leaders. In the New Testament we find that Jesus was found guilty, even though he was innocent and without sin. Matthew 26:67–68 explains the details of this abuse. "Then they spat in His face and beat Him; and others struck Him with the palms of their hands." Even though Matthew does not independently state that the Romans tore out the beard of Jesus, Roman tradition suggests that it would have happened. To insult a prisoner, Roman centurions would mock him by shaving or pulling out his beard. It was even more amusing to do this to a Jewish man, because of their customs and beliefs.

While researching the way the Romans punished their criminals, I had to call it torture. The Jewish law demanded no more than thirty-nine lashes. This was done because it was known that forty lashes could lead to death. Romans, however, were beyond cruel. There were no limits on the times a man received the whip. Even if the prisoner would faint or fall, the guards would pick him up and continue the beatings. If criminals died during the beating, it saved time from having to crucify them. Those who survived had bodies that were destroyed. Many times, their skin was left hanging off of them, blood pouring to the ground.

When the Romans beat Jesus, he was treated as every other criminal would be treated. He, though, was treated a bit more cruelly. They slapped him, spit on him, and then formed a crown out of sharp thorns and jammed it on his head. They were mocking him because he was supposed to be the King of the Jews.

This treatment led to a man who was unrecognizable as a man. His face and body would have been distorted. The prophet Isaiah described the beating in Isa 52:14: "So His appearance was marred more than any man and His form more than the sons of men."

Jesus' suffering would go even further than the insults, beatings, and hair pulling. After Pilate released Barabbas, instead of Jesus, Matt 27:26–30, 35 told us that Pontius Pilate "released he Barabbas unto them: and when he had scourged Jesus, he delivered him to be crucified. Then the soldiers of the governor took Jesus into the common hall, and gathered unto him the whole band of soldiers. And they stripped him, and put on him a scarlet robe. And when they had platted a crown of thorns, they put it upon his head, and a reed in his right hand: and they bowed the knee before him, and mocked him, saying, Hail, King of the Jews! And they spit upon him, and took the reed, and smote him on the head." The prophet Micah explained how Jesus would be struck with a rod. Although the prophet Micah was foretelling of "Bethlehem Ephrathah, though you are small among the clans of Judah, out of you will come for me one who will be ruler over Israel, whose origins are from of old from ancient times." In Mic 5:1, it is written, "A siege is laid against us. They will strike Israel's ruler on the cheek with a rod." As we read, they abused Jesus so greatly, he was unrecognizable.

Jesus withstood it all. The pain and suffering were taken for one purpose. He was fulfilling the will of God so that many would be saved. Jesus suffered and bore the abuse for us: it was for our physical and spiritual healing. Isaiah 53:4–5 shows us that "surely he took up our pain and bore our suffering, yet we considered him punished by God, stricken by him, and afflicted. But he was pierced for our transgressions, he was crushed for our iniquities; the punishment that brought us peace was on him, and by his wounds we are healed." Matthew justifies Isaiah's prophecy. In Matt 8:17 he writes, "He took up our infirmities and bore our diseases." The apostle Paul and his disciple Sosthenes in 1 Cor 15:1–3 further Isaiah's words by writing, "Now, brothers and sisters, I want to remind you of the gospel I preached to you, which you received and on which you have taken your stand. By this gospel you are saved, if you hold firmly to the word I preached to you. Otherwise, you have believed in vain. For what I received I passed on to you as of first importance: that Christ died for our sins according to the Scriptures" and according to the prophecies.

This Son of God, who came as a servant, was as a lamb that does not defend itself. Isaiah 53:7 describes this. "He was oppressed and afflicted, yet he did not open his mouth; he was led like a lamb to the slaughter, and as a sheep before its shearers is silent, so he did not open his mouth." Matthew 27:12 stated the prophesier's fulfillment. "When he was accused by the chief priests and the elders, he gave no answer."

After the conviction, Jesus was to be crucified. The Old Testament Psalms try to describe the form of punishment Jesus would go through, even though crucifixions had not been used yet. In Ps 22:14–15, David says, "I am poured out like water, and all my bones are out of joint. My heart has turned to wax; it has melted within me. My mouth is dried up like a potsherd, and my tongue sticks to the roof of my mouth; you lay me in the dust of death." In verses 16 and 17 he further describes the suffering, writing, "They pierce my hands and my feet. All my bones are on display; people stare and gloat over me." This prophecy was satisfied when John wrote, in John 19:16–18, a description that defines the song of David. "Finally Pilate handed him over to them to be crucified. So the soldiers took charge of Jesus. Carrying his own cross, he went out to the place of the Skull (which in Aramaic is called Golgotha). There they crucified him." While on the cross, Jesus makes seven statements. The first words were "Father, forgive them, for they know not what they do" (Luke 23:34). When one of the others crucified with him asked for Jesus to remember him when the Christ arrived in his kingdom, Jesus said, "Today, you will be with me in paradise" (Luke 23:43). Looking down on his mother and his disciple John, Jesus spoke, "Woman, behold your son: behold your mother" (John 19:26–27). In obvious agony Jesus shouted to his Father in heaven, "My God, my God, why have you forsaken me?" (Mark 15:34). Seemingly fulfilling another prophecy, Jesus acknowledged, "I thirst" (John 19:28). Finally, with his last two breaths, he said, "It is finished" (John 19:30), and "Father, into your hands I commend my spirit" (Luke 23:46).

During his time on the cross, though, he fulfilled other prophecies. What David sang in his psalms, Jesus did. Psalm 22, the song of David, is one of the most convincing psalms in the Old Testament when it comes to fulfilling prophecy. The life of David, in many ways, was a mirror to the life of Jesus. David ran into tormentors who teased him. Psalm 22:7 shows this. Davis said, "All who see me mock me; they hurl insults, shaking their heads." Luke 23:35 indeed reflects this. "The people stood by and watched; the rulers, meanwhile, sneered at him and said, 'He saved others, let him save himself if he is the chosen one, the Messiah of God.'" In Ps 22:18, David writes, "They divide my clothes among them and cast lots for my garment." John 19:23–24 completes this. "When the soldiers crucified Jesus, they took his clothes, dividing them into four shares, one for each of them, with the undergarment remaining. This garment was seamless, woven in one piece from top to bottom. 'Let's not tear it,' they said to one another. 'Let's decide by lot who will get it.' This happened that the scripture might be fulfilled that said, 'They divided my clothes among them and cast lots for my garment.' So this is what the soldiers did."

Jesus died on the cross between two criminals (the Hebrew word for "transgressors"). Isaiah stated this in chapter 53, verse 12. "He poured out Himself to death, and was numbered with the transgressors; Yet He Himself bore the sin of many, and interceded for the transgressors." Matthew 27:38 tells the completion of this prophecy. "Then two robbers were crucified with Him, one on the right and another on the left." Luke wrote in his Gospel, 23:32–33, that Jesus was killed between two criminals. "Two others, both criminals, were led out to be executed with him. When they came to a place called the Skull, they nailed him to the cross. And the criminals were also crucified—one on his right and one on his left."

While Jesus hung between the two criminals he said, "I thirst." In response, a Roman mocked Jesus by offering him vinegar and gall soaked on a sponge. Matthew, Mark, Luke, and John all commented on this. Matthew wrote, "The soldiers gave Jesus wine mixed with bitter gall, but when he had tasted it, he refused to drink it" (Matt 27:34). Mark said, "They offered him wine drugged with myrrh, but he refused it" (Mark 15:23). Luke followed by stating, "The soldiers mocked him, too, by offering him a drink of sour wine" (Luke 23:36). John descriptively said, "A jar of sour wine was sitting there, so they soaked a sponge in it, put it on a hyssop branch, and held it up to his lips" (John 19:29). All four disciples mirrored in their Gospels what David talked about what he was being fed by his enemies. In Ps 69:21, David prayed to God about his enemies and said, "If only one person would show some pity; if only one would turn and comfort me. But instead, they give me poison for food; they offer me sour wine for my thirst." At one point, David cried out to the Lord. He shouted, "My God, my God, why have you abandoned me? Why are you so far away when I groan for help?" (Ps 22:1). Jesus too cried out on the cross. "At about three o'clock, Jesus called out with a loud voice, 'Eli, Eli, lema sabachthani?' which means 'My God, my God, why have you abandoned me?'" (Matt 27:46).

Jesus' work was almost complete . . . almost. Just before he died he spoke. Luke 23:46 tell us the words: "And when Jesus had cried out with a loud voice, He said, 'Father, into Your hands I commit My spirit.' Having said this, He breathed His last." David had used the same words in Ps 31:5. "Into Your hand I commit my spirit; You have redeemed me, O Lord God of truth." With David's prophecy realized, the body of the Messiah was dead.

In those days, because a crucifixion was a long, slow death, many prisoners would not die on the same day they were crucified. It was the rule of thumb that the Romans would break the feet of the condemned. They would not be able to use any foot or leg muscles to hold themselves up on the cross, and they would thereby suffocate to death. They were going to do this to Jesus but, according to the Gospels, the centurion guarding Jesus took a spear and thrust it into the side of the Christ, and immediately blood and water came out. He told the others the man was dead, so they did not need to break his bones. At that moment the earth shook. The centurion, who had watched all of this and felt the earthquake, was terrified, but felt a change in himself. He exclaimed, "Surely he was the Son of God!" (Matt 27:54). This fulfilled the law in the Old Testament. It was the rule that the Jews could not break the bones of the Passover lamb. Numbers 9:12 explained the law of the Passover lamb. It read: "They must not leave any of it till morning or break any of its bones. When they celebrate the Passover, they must follow all the regulations." Jesus was now the Passover Lamb that was a sacrifice for all mankind.

At the hour the soul of Jesus left the body, the sky had already become dark over the entire land. It was as if a complete eclipse had occurred. Luke 23:44–45 expresses that "now it was about the sixth hour, and there was darkness over all the earth until the ninth hour. Then the sun was darkened, and the veil of the temple was torn in two." It is interesting that darkness was experienced when God was about to perform a miracle. It was God who was preparing the people of Israel for freedom. Exodus 10:21–23 tells of the time when God told Moses, "Stretch out your hand toward the sky so that darkness spreads over Egypt—darkness that can be felt." The Jews were about to be freed from slavery and the Egyptians. The darkness at the death of the Messiah, in a way, signified freedom. Jesus suffered for us so believers would be free from the eternal death required because of our sins. Although this is not a direct prophecy, the correlation is amazing.

During this darkness the curtain in the temple was torn in two. Freedom had been given to man, and we didn't even realize it. In the Old Testament, the temple was a place of division. It separated the people in the temple from the holy of holies, where God reigned. Leviticus 16:2 says, "The Lord said to Moses: 'Tell your brother Aaron that he is not to come whenever he chooses into the Most Holy Place behind the curtain in front of the atonement cover on the ark, or else he will die.'" Leviticus explains that God would appear in the holy of holies. Then, there was a need for a curtain to separate God from man. With the tearing of the curtain, there was no longer a division between man and God. Hebrews 4:14 says, "Therefore, since we have a great high priest who has ascended into heaven, Jesus the Son of God, let us hold firmly to the faith we profess." And in Heb 10:19–20 we find that "we have confidence to enter the Most Holy Place by the blood of Jesus by a new and living way opened for us through the curtain, that is, his body." With the tearing of Jesus' flesh, as the tearing of the curtain in the temple, we can now realize there is no longer a division between God and man, thanks to Jesus.

The Romans released the body of Christ, and according to prophecy two other events happened. First, Jesus was buried on the same day he died. Remember that the Old Testament, in Numbers, stated that the Passover lamb was not to be kept overnight. The second event fulfilled Isaiah's prophecy. He spoke the word of God, foretelling that Jesus was to be buried in a rich man's tomb. "He was assigned a grave with the wicked, and with the rich in his death, though he had done no violence, nor was any deceit in his mouth" (Isa 53:9). Isaiah's words were realized when, according to John in his Gospel, a rich believer,

> Joseph of Arimathea asked Pilate for the body of Jesus. Now Joseph was a disciple of Jesus, but secretly because he feared the Jewish leaders. With Pilate's permission, he came and took the body away. He was accompanied by Nicodemus, the man who earlier had visited Jesus at night. Nicodemus brought a mixture of myrrh and aloes, about seventy-five pounds. Taking Jesus' body, the two of them wrapped it, with the spices, in strips of linen. This was in accordance with Jewish burial customs. At the place where Jesus was crucified, there was a garden, and in the garden a new tomb, in which no one had ever been laid. Because it was the Jewish day of Preparation and since the tomb was nearby, they laid Jesus there. (John 19:38–42)

There were many times in my life when I asked, Why? Why did Jesus die? What purpose was it to serve? After reading both Matt 13:31–35 and Lev 23:6, I realized that Jesus was like unleavened bread and a seed planted in the ground. We know that bread is not finished until it has risen, and we know a seed must rise from the ground to produce anything. This parable began to explain the resurrection and the kingdom of God.

Unleavened bread is a reminder to the Jews that God quickly freed them from slavery in Egypt, so quickly they couldn't wait for yeast to work. Leviticus 23:6 states, "On the fifteenth day of that month the Lord's Festival of Unleavened Bread begins; for seven days you must eat bread made without yeast." Jesus, not yet finished with his work on earth, told his disciples about the kingdom of heaven and how it was like that seed and leavened bread. Jesus explained in a parable, "'The kingdom of heaven is like a mustard seed, which a man took and planted in his field. Though it is the smallest of all seeds, yet when it grows, it is the largest of garden plants and becomes a tree, so that the birds come and perch in its branches.' He told them still another parable: 'The kingdom of heaven is like yeast that a woman took and mixed into about sixty pounds of flour until it worked all through the dough'" (Matt 13:31–35). Jesus told parables to the crowd and his disciples so they could better understand his words. The Old Testament fulfilled yet another prophecy spoken through the prophet David: "I will open my mouth in parables, I will utter things hidden since the creation of the world" (Ps 78:2).

Since a seed will never be a plant until it comes up from the ground and since bread needs yeast to rise, then the message of Jesus rising eventually explains what heaven is and gives me the reason why he died. John 12:24 states, "Very truly I tell you, unless a kernel of wheat falls to the ground and dies, it remains only a single seed. But if it dies, it produces many seeds." Jesus was now the bread and the seed. He died to save us all, and he had told us that he would rise again in three days.

This suffering servant took on our sins and died. He was the good shepherd, and God allowed him to suffer for his lost sheep. Isaiah 53:6 foretold of the sacrifice of Jesus this way: "We all, like sheep, have gone astray, each of us has turned to our own way; and the LORD has laid on him the iniquity of us all." The prophecy was fulfilled in Rom 4:23–25. "Now it was not written for his sake alone that it was imputed to him, but also for us. It shall be imputed to us who believe in Him who raised up Jesus our Lord from the dead, who was delivered up because of our offenses, and was raised because of our justification." I have stated before that Isa 53 was one of the most prophetic chapters in the Old Testament telling of the Messiah, Jesus. Isaiah described what this suffering servant did for the sins of others. Isaiah in 53:10 was prophesying that the Messiah would "render Himself as a guilt offering on behalf of Israel and that His sacrifice will please the LORD." Because of the death of Jesus, this sacrifice would atonement for the sins of mankind.

It was Jesus, then, who fulfilled the words of the prophet by dying on the cross. He fulfilled the following:

> Yet it pleased the Lord to bruise Him; He has put Him to grief. When You make His soul an offering for sin, He shall see His seed, He shall prolong His days, and the pleasure of the Lord shall prosper in His hand. He shall see the labor of His soul, and be satisfied. By His knowledge My righteous Servant shall justify many, for He shall bear their iniquities. Therefore I will divide Him a portion with the great, and He shall divide the spoil with the strong, because He poured out His soul unto death, and He was numbered with the transgressors, and He bore the sin of many, and made intercession for the transgressors. (Isa 53:10–12)

The Old has foretold the New!

Chapter 7

AFTER THE RESURRECTION

REMEMBER THE STORY OF JONAH? In chapter 1, verse 17 we find out, "Now the Lord provided a huge fish to swallow Jonah, and Jonah was in the belly of the fish three days and three nights." Matthew 12:40 described this comparison in this way: "For as Jonah was three days and three nights in the belly of a huge fish, so the Son of Man will be three days and three nights in the heart of the earth." He died and was laid in the tomb, but he was not finished.

Jesus was dead and buried, and on the third day he rose from the dead. In Ps 17:15, David sings to the Lord. It is a prediction of the resurrection: "As for me, I will be vindicated and will see your face; when I awake, I will be satisfied with seeing your likeness." David is prophesying to us that he should be satisfied with the image of God, when he, Jesus, rises from the dead. Luke 24:6 explains David's words. "He is not here, but has risen. Remember how he told you, while he was still in Galilee."

From the beginning, people believed that God would rescue them from death, or at least they hoped so. King David knew without a doubt that God would rescue him from death. He believed that there was a life after death with his God. It was because he always atoned for the sins he committed, he believed. In Ps 49:15 David believed, "But God will redeem me from the realm of the dead; he will surely take me to himself." Isaiah actually prophesied the resurrection in chapter 5 verse 8 when he said, "He will swallow up death forever. The Sovereign Lord will wipe away the tears from all faces; he will remove his people's disgrace from all the earth. The Lord has spoken."

Psalm 40:2–5 tells us about the joy that David felt when God rescued him.

> He lifted me out of the slimy pit, out of the mud and mire; he set my feet on a rock and gave me a firm place to stand. He put a new song in my mouth, a hymn of praise to our God. Many will see and fear the Lord and put their trust in him. Blessed is the one who trusts in the Lord, who does not look to the proud, to those who turn aside to false gods. Many, Lord my God, are the wonders you have done, the things you planned for us. None can compare with you; were I to speak and tell of your deeds, they would be too many to declare.

This song expresses that God did not just see what David was going through. He didn't just hear David pray. He acted upon it! He lifted David out of that pit, foreshadowing what Jesus was going to do for us. David had faith, believed, kept hope, and continued to pray.

The Messiah, after facing the misery of the grave and the agony in garden and the cross (his slimy pit and miry clay) appeared to Mary and his disciples. Jesus proved that those who endure will eventually feel exceeding joy. John 20:20 describes, then, that joy. "After he said this, he showed them his hands and side. The disciples were overjoyed when they saw the Lord." This event of the resurrection was told by Matthew, Mark, Luke, and John in the Gospels. *Gospel*, translated from the Greek word *euangelion*, means "good news" or "good tidings." The good news in the New Testament was about Jesus, the Messiah, dying and taking our sin upon himself.

Just as God took David to himself after his death, and just as Isaiah had prophecies that the Messiah would swallow up death, God resurrected Jesus three days after his crucifixion. Mark 16:1–7 explains the life after the death of Jesus.

> When the Sabbath was over, Mary Magdalene, Mary the mother of James, and Salome bought spices so that they might go to anoint Jesus' body. Very early on the first day of the week, just after sunrise, they were on their way to the tomb and they asked each other, "Who will roll the stone away from the entrance of the tomb?" But when they looked up, they saw that the stone, which was very large, had been rolled away. As they entered the tomb, they saw a young man dressed in a white robe sitting on the right side, and they were alarmed. "Don't be alarmed," he said. "You are looking for Jesus the Nazarene, who was crucified. He has risen! He is not here. See the place where they laid him. But go, tell his disciples

and Peter, 'He is going ahead of you into Galilee. There you will see him, just as he told you.'"

When Paul wrote his letter to the people of Corinth, he explained to them how and when Jesus appeared to many after his death and resurrection. For forty days, hundreds of people saw Jesus appear among them. He had truly risen from the dead and wanted to allow people to know without any doubt. By dying and rising again, as we have stated, according to the Gospels, Jesus first appeared to Mary. John 20:11–16 records the following.

> Now Mary stood outside the tomb crying. As she wept, she bent over to look into the tomb and saw two angels in white, seated where Jesus' body had been, one at the head and the other at the foot. They asked her, "Woman, why are you crying?" "They have taken my Lord away," she said, "and I don't know where they have put him." At this, she turned around and saw Jesus standing there, but she did not realize that it was Jesus. He asked her, "Woman, why are you crying? Who is it you are looking for?" Thinking he was the gardener, she said, "Sir, if you have carried him away, tell me where you have put him, and I will get him." Jesus said to her, "Mary." She turned toward him and cried out in Aramaic, "Rabboni!"

Jesus was seen by so many after he rose from the dead. Jesus appeared to Cleopas and one other disciple, but "their eyes were holden" so that they could not recognize him.

> Now that same day two of them were going to a village called Emmaus, about seven miles from Jerusalem. They were talking with each other about everything that had happened. As they talked and discussed these things with each other, Jesus himself came up and walked along with them; but they were kept from recognizing him. He asked them, "What are you discussing together as you walk along?" They stood still, their faces downcast. One of them, named Cleopas, asked him, "Are you the only one visiting Jerusalem who does not know the things that have happened there in these days?"
>
> "What things?" he asked. Surprised by this man's question, they explained. "About Jesus of Nazareth," they replied. "He was a prophet, powerful in word and deed before God and all the people. The chief priests and our rulers handed him over to be sentenced to death, and they crucified him; but we had hoped that he was the one who was going to redeem Israel. And what is more, it is the third day since all this took place. In addition, some of our women

amazed us. They went to the tomb early this morning but didn't find his body. They came and told us that they had seen a vision of angels, who said he was alive. Then some of our companions went to the tomb and found it just as the women had said, but they did not see Jesus." He said to them, "How foolish you are, and how slow to believe all that the prophets have spoken! Did not the Messiah have to suffer these things and then enter his glory?" And beginning with Moses and all the Prophets, he explained to them what was said in all the Scriptures concerning himself. As they approached the village to which they were going, Jesus continued on as if he were going farther. They still did not know who he was. But, they urged him strongly, "Stay with us, for it is nearly evening; the day is almost over."

So he went in to stay with them. When he was at the table, he took bread, gave thanks, broke it and began to give it to them. Then their eyes were opened and they recognized him, and he disappeared from their sight. They asked each other, "Were not our hearts burning within us while he talked with us on the road and opened the Scriptures to us?" They got up and returned at once to Jerusalem. There they found the Eleven and those with them, assembled together and saying, "It is true! The Lord has risen and has appeared to Simon." (Luke 24:13–34)

Later, Jesus did appear to the disciples at different times. Matthew 28:16 describes the meeting. "But the eleven disciples proceeded to Galilee, to the mountain which Jesus had designated. When they saw Him, they worshiped Him; but some were doubtful. And Jesus came up and spoke to them, saying, 'All authority has been given to Me in heaven and on earth.'"

Mark, in 16:14–16, simply saw it this way: "Later Jesus appeared to the Eleven as they were eating; he rebuked them for their lack of faith and their stubborn refusal to believe those who had seen him after he had risen. He said to them, 'Go into all the world and preach the gospel to all creation. Whoever believes and is baptized will be saved, but whoever does not believe will be condemned.'" Luke, on the other hand described the meeting as ghostly.

While they were still talking about this, Jesus himself stood among them and said to them, "Peace be with you." They were startled and frightened, thinking they saw a ghost. He said to them, "Why are you troubled, and why do doubts rise in your minds? Look at my hands and my feet. It is I myself! Touch me and see; a ghost does not have flesh and bones, as you see I have." When he had said this, he showed them his hands and feet. And while they still did not believe it because of joy and amazement, he asked them, "Do you have anything here to eat?" They gave him a piece of broiled fish, and he took it and ate it in their presence. He said to them, "This is what I told you while I was still with you: Everything must be fulfilled that is written about me in the Law of Moses, the Prophets and the Psalms." Then he opened their minds so they could under-stand the Scriptures. He told them, "This is what is written: The Messiah will suffer and rise from the dead on the third day, and repentance for the forgiveness of sins will be preached in his name to all nations, beginning at Jerusalem. You are witnesses of these things. I am going to send you what my Father has promised; but stay in the city until you have been clothed with power from on high." (Luke 24:36–49)

Finally, John wrote of a meeting occurring one week later than the other. He stated, in John 20:26–31, "A week later his disciples were in the house again, and Thomas was with them. Though the doors were locked, Jesus came and stood among them and said, 'Peace be with you!' Then he said to Thomas, 'Put your finger here; see my hands. Reach out your hand and put it into my side. Stop doubting and believe.' Thomas said to him, 'My Lord and my God!' Then Jesus told him, 'Because you have seen me, you have believed; blessed are those who have not seen and yet have believed.'" In 1 Cor 15:3–8, Paul discussed the resurrection. He wrote:

> For what I received I passed on to you as of first importance: that Christ died for our sins according to the Scriptures, that he was buried, that he was raised on the third day according to the Scrip-tures, and that he appeared to Cephas, and then to the Twelve. After that, he appeared to more than five hundred of the brothers and sisters at the same time, most of whom are still living, though some have fallen asleep. Then he appeared to James, then to all the apostles, and last of all he appeared to me also, as to one abnor-mally born.

Saying that he, Paul, was abnormally born refers to the fact that he was spiritually dead when he saw Jesus and became a Christian.

In Acts 9:3 Saul, who became Paul after his conversion, wrote about the time he neared Damascus on his journey: "Suddenly a light from heav-en flashed around him. He fell to the ground and heard a voice say to him, 'Saul, Saul, why do you persecute me?' 'Who are you, Lord?' Saul asked. 'I am Jesus, whom you are persecuting,' he replied." Paul was converted to Christianity and began his mission for the Messiah.

If these were the only people who had written about the resurrection of the Messiah, then we could simply state it was the followers of Jesus only who believed He was a risen Lord. Paul, though, had been on a mission to kill Christians. Before his conversion to Christianity, Paul was known by his birth name, Saul. He was well educated and even learning to become a rabbi. Saul was fervent in his Jewish faith and was extremely hostile toward the new Christian followers of Christ. He hated them and had no problem seeing them dead. His heart was hardened, and he didn't believe in the good news about Jesus being the Messiah. He rebuked these Christians with this false message and considered them to be a threat to his beliefs. Acts 8:3 shows his feelings. "But Saul began to destroy the church. Going from house to house, he dragged off both men and women and put them in prison."

When Saul met Jesus on the road to Damascus, he was converted and became one of the strongest Christians of his day. He explained how he had gone from a man who "persecuted the followers of this Way [Christians] to their death, arresting both men and women and throwing them into prison, as the high priest and all the Council can themselves testify. I even obtained letters from them to their associates in Damascus and went there to bring these people as prisoners to Jerusalem to be punished" (Acts 22:4–5). By telling this, and by showing how he had changed, he helped others know Jesus, the resurrected Messiah.

If, again, these were the only people who recorded the resurrected Christ, then this would be a story from secondary sources only. However, this is not the case. There were three leaders of the early church named Clement of Rome, Polycarp, and Ignatius who mention Jesus' resurrection. Although two of them knew Peter and John, they were not disciples or apostles and are considered primary sources of the events of the first century AD. Clement of Rome became a follower of Jesus. He wrote that Jesus was who he claimed to be and that Jesus died and rose again. He wrote, "Having been fully assured through the resurrection[1] of our Lord Jesus Christ and confirmed in the word of God . . . they [the first Christians] went forth with the glad tidings that the kingdom of God should come." Clement witnessed to others, even when he was imprisoned by Emperor Trajan, about the resurrection of Jesus. When he wrote about resurrection

---

1. Dickerson, "Clement of Rome."

and the phoenix rising from the ashes, he said, "Do we then think it to be a great and marvelous thing, if the Creator of the universe shall bring about the resurrection of them that have served Him with holiness in the assurance of a good faith, seeing that He showeth to us even by a bird the magnificence of His promise?"[2]

Polycarp, AD 69–155, believed that the believers in Christ would be raised up as Jesus was. He wrote a letter to the church of Philippi saying, "Serve the Lord in fear and truth, as those who have forsaken the vain empty talk and error of the multitude. Believe in Him who was raised up, our Lord Jesus Christ, from the dead."[3] So, Polycarp was also a primary source concerning the resurrection. He was alive during that time and mentioned how Jesus had risen from the dead.

Ignatius was the third source believing that Christians will rise from the dead just as Jesus rose. Ignatius said, "For I know that after His resurrection also He was still possessed of flesh, and I believe that He is so now." In his second chapter, he wrote, "Now, He suffered all these things for our sake, that we might be saved. And He suffered truly, even as also He truly raised up Himself, not, as certain unbelievers maintain, that He only seemed to suffer, as they themselves only seem to be [Christians]. And as they believe, so shall it happen unto them, when they shall be divested of their bodies, and be mere evil spirits."[4]

The disciples and apostles were, then, not the only people to write about Jesus. Those who did not write biblical text were convinced that Jesus not only was a virtuous man with followers but possessed supernatural powers, performed supernatural feats, and was considered the person that he claimed to be. He was the Messiah.

2. Kirby, "First Clement," 1 Clem 26:1.

3. Polycarp, "Epistle of Polycarp."

4. Kirby, "Ignatius to the Smyrnaeans."

Chapter 8

THE ASCENSION

FORTY DAYS AFTER THE RESURRECTION, Jesus told his disciples to remain in Jerusalem so that they could receive the power of the Holy Spirit. He was then taken into heaven. Two men in white robes told them that Jesus would return, "in the same way you have seen him go into heaven" (Acts 1:11). The act of going to heaven was not a new concept for the Jews. The Old Testament describes what happened to both Enoch and Elijah, two men who pleased God.

Enoch was an example of how a person was to love God and how God loved that believer. Genesis 5 describes that "after he became the father of Methuselah, Enoch walked faithfully with God for 300 years" (Gen 5:22–24). Paul wrote in Hebrews, "By faith Enoch was taken up so that he should not see death, and he was not found, be cause God had taken him. Now before he was taken he was commended as having pleased God" (Heb 11:5). His life was an example of how a believer in Yahweh was to act. He was also a prophet who mirrored the rapture of the saints. In the end times, Christians will be taken from the earth. The dead will be resurrected first, but the living believers will be taken up to meet Jesus in the clouds. Enoch prophesied, "Behold the Lord cometh with ten thousand of his saints, to execute judgment upon all and to convince all that are ungodly among them of all their ungodly deeds" (Jude 1:15). Enoch, the great-grandfather of Noah, was taken by God so that he could escape death. Enoch was holy while most of the rest of the world had fallen into sin, disobeyed the Lord, and had become immoral and evil.

The story of Elijah is found in the Old Testament and describes a time when the kings of Israel had become evil. God sent Elijah to tell the Jews how they were to eliminate their suffering and immorality. Elijah became the only prophet of God left in the world, because all the other prophets and kings had turned to worshiping Baal, the god of the Canaanites and Phoenicians. This prophet came to show them the way to return to Yahweh. Elijah, then, was reflecting the coming of Jesus to save his children from sin. Elijah showed the Israelites that they could not serve two gods. Matthew, in Matt 6:24, said, "No man can serve two masters: for either he will hate the one, and love the other; or else he will hold to the one, and despise the other."

Both Enoch and Elijah ascended into heaven, and when Jesus was about to do the same, he spoke to his disciples. Acts 1:6–11 tells the story.

> Then they gathered around him and asked him, "Lord, are you at this time going to restore the kingdom to Israel?" He said to them: "It is not for you to know the times or dates the Father has set by his own authority. But you will receive power when the Holy Spirit comes on you; and you will be my witnesses in Jerusalem, and in all Judea and Samaria, and to the ends of the earth." After he said this, he was taken up before their very eyes, and a cloud hid him from their sight. They were looking intently up into the sky as he was going, when suddenly two men dressed in white stood beside them. "Men of Galilee," they said, "why do you stand here looking into the sky? This same Jesus, who has been taken from you into heaven, will come back in the same way you have seen him go into heaven."

Mark completed his remarks by stating, "After the Lord Jesus had spoken to them, he was taken up into heaven and he sat at the right hand of God" (Mark 16:19). Although Matthew, Mark, and John spoke of the ascension, Luke and Paul, in the book of Acts, explained the event more precisely. The ascension and the promise of the return were a fulfillment of prophecy. When Peter wrote, in 1 Pet 3:22, about Jesus sitting at the right hand of God, he may as well have been explaining the song David sang. Peter said, "Now Christ has gone to heaven. He is seated in the place of honor next to God, and all the angels and authorities and powers accept his authority." The Old Testament prophet David told of this coming event. In Ps 110:1 David sang, "The Lord said to my lord: 'Sit at my right hand until I make your enemies a footstool for your feet.'" When defining "the Lord said to my

'Lord,'" the first "lord" is Yahweh, God Almighty. The second "Lord" is the Messiah, the Christ.

In another psalm, the prophet wrote, "Thou hast ascended on high, thou hast led captivity captive: Thou hast received gifts for men; Yea, for the rebellious also, that the Lord GOD might dwell among them" (Ps 68:18). David was actually recording God's ascension to Mount Zion and observing the past victories. He was also describing future victories that will be won by God from heaven. Paul also used David's psalm when describing the ascension of Jesus. In Eph 4:8, he wrote:

> Unto every one of us is given grace according to the measure of the gift of Christ. Wherefore he saith, When he ascended up on high, he led captivity captive, and gave gifts unto men. Now that he ascended, what is it but that he also descended first into the lower parts of the earth? He that descended is the same also that ascended up far above all heavens, that he might fill all things. And he gave some, apostles; and some, prophets; and some, evangelists; and some, pastors and teachers; for the perfecting of the saints, for the work of the ministry, for the edifying of the body of Christ.

The ascension of the Messiah is not only predicted in the Old Testament. Jesus, himself, prophesied the ascension. John records a time when Jesus was talking to Nicodemus. Jesus told Nicodemus in John 3:12–13, "I have spoken to you of earthly things and you do not believe; how then will you believe if I speak of heavenly things? No one has ever gone into heaven except the one who came from heaven—the Son of Man." When Jesus claimed that no one ascended unless they actually came from heaven, he was not rejecting the fact that Enoch and Elijah also ascended to heaven. All three ascended, but Jesus had died. We remember that Enoch and Elijah never saw death, so Jesus was actually stating that he was "lifted up" from the dead. The difference, then, is that Jesus came from heaven, was born a man, was crucified and died, was resurrected, and then ascended. John furthers the prophecy in chapter 6, verse 62. Jesus was describing to many followers how the Israelites were fed bread in the desert. He told them that whoever fed on "this bread," meaning him, would live forever. The crowd was confused and found the teaching too hard. Jesus said to them, "Does this offend you? Then what if you see the Son of Man ascend to where he was before! The Spirit gives life; the flesh counts for nothing. The words I have spoken to you—they are full of the Spirit and life." Then they were soon to see Jesus ascend.

In John 16:5, Jesus was speaking to his disciples and explaining what they would suffer when he was gone. They were full of grief but did not question where he was going. Jesus said, "I have told you this, so that when their time comes you will remember that I warned you about them. I did not tell you this from the beginning because I was with you, but now I am going to him who sent me. None of you asks me, 'Where are you going?'" Jesus was about to ascend to his Father in heaven. Then, Jesus told them why he was leaving. In John 14:1–4, the Christ had told them, "Do not let your hearts be troubled. You believe in God; believe also in me. My Father's house has many rooms; if that were not so, would I have told you that I am going there to prepare a place for you? And if I go and prepare a place for you, I will come back and take you to be with me that you also may be where I am. You know the way to the place where I am going." The ascension was the action that now allowed the disciples and apostles to begin spreading the gospel of Christ. It had been told by the prophets of the Old Testament and the disciples who wrote the New Testament and was a personal word given them by the Messiah, himself. It was also the beginning of the end, because it is from heaven that Jesus will return. Daniel explained it all when he wrote Dan 7:13–14. There, he was explaining that the ascension of Christ would fulfill his prophecy. Daniel prophesied, "In my vision at night I looked, and there before me was one like a son of man, coming with the clouds of heaven. He approached the Ancient of Days and was led into his presence. He was given authority, glory and sovereign power; all nations and peoples of every language worshiped him. His dominion is an everlasting dominion that will not pass away, and his kingdom is one that will never be destroyed."

Most of the time we read about the ascension and just accept it as fact. But why did Jesus ascend? Why not stay on earth and claim his kingdom at that time? According to the word of God, Jesus ascended into heaven for many reasons. First, he did this to show completion of salvation. When we finish work, many times the first thing we do is to sit and look over the work we have completed. Hebrews 10:12–13 explained, "But when Christ had offered for all time a single sacrifice for sins, he sat down at the right hand of God, waiting from that time until his enemies should be made a footstool for his feet." The second reason is the Messiah's intercession on behalf of us. Jesus went to heaven to intercede for humanity as the eternal high priest. Hebrews 7:2 tells us, "Therefore he is able to save completely those who come to God through him, because he always lives to intercede for them."

Hebrews 4:14–16 is precisely why the High Priest, Jesus, ascended. It tells us "since we have a great high priest who has ascended into heaven, Jesus the Son of God, let us hold firmly to the faith we profess. For we do not have a high priest who is unable to empathize with our weaknesses, but we have one who has been tempted in every way, just as we are—yet he did not sin. Let us then approach God's throne of grace with confidence, so that we may receive mercy and find grace to help us in our time of need." Jesus was fulfilling the prophecy of Daniel, who said, "You will see the Son of Man seated at the right hand of power." This shows his authority and ability to go to the Father in the name of the believers. Another reason Jesus ascended was to accept his triumphant coronation. In 1 Tim 6:13–15 Jesus is called "the blessed and only Sovereign, the King of kings and Lord of lords" and fulfills the prophecy found in the vision of Dan 7:14. "He was given authority, glory and sovereign power; all nations and peoples of every language worshiped him. His dominion is an everlasting dominion that will not pass away, and his kingdom is one that will never be destroyed." Jesus, preparing for the power of the Holy Spirit to come to his chosen, ascended to heaven. He had told his disciples in John 16:7, "Nevertheless I tell you the truth, it is expedient for you that I go away: for if I go not away, the Comforter will not come to you; but if I depart, I will send him to you." If he had not gone to heaven, his followers would not have received the power to complete their mission of spreading the gospel. In fact it was not fitting that Jesus remain, both for our sake and for who he was, is, and will always be. Jesus ascended into heaven to begin his reign in glory, but he didn't abandon us. On the contrary, he said, "I am with you always, to the close of the age" (Matt 28:20).

Even the author of Prov 30:3–4 said, "Neither have I learned wisdom, nor do I have the knowledge of the Holy One. Who has ascended into heaven and descended? Who has gathered the wind in His fists? Who has wrapped the waters in His garment? Who has established all the ends of the earth? What is His name or His son's name? Surely you know!" This entire proverb prophesied what we know today. We, as Christians, accept and acknowledge that God and his Son, Jesus, have ascended into heaven.

Chapter 9

ATONEMENT

ALL OF THE PEOPLE who realized that Jesus was now in heaven and preparing a place for them soon began to preach his message. God had sent his only Son to take away the sins of mankind by dying on the cross and, even more importantly, rising from the dead to show us all that we, too, could have everlasting life. Romans 6:23 simply says, "For the wages of sin is death, but the free gift of God is eternal life in Christ Jesus our Lord." The prophets warned the people of their sins long ago. Ezekiel, in chapter 18, verse 4, wrote, "Behold, all souls are mine; the soul of the father as well as the soul of the son is mine: the soul who sins shall die." Before Jesus, the Old Testament Jews had to give sacrifices to atone for their sins. Although sacrifice is not practiced today, the feast of first fruits in Lev 23:10 prophetically describes Jesus as the first fruit from the dead. It explained, "Speak to the Israelites and say to them: 'When you enter the land I am going to give you and you reap its harvest, bring to the priest a sheaf of the first grain you harvest.'" Actually, Leviticus describes the need to bring the first grain, the first and best fruits, and the perfect goat or bull as a sacrifice for the sins of the Israelites. When discussing the resurrection of the Christ, in 1 Cor 15:20, the author calls the Messiah the first fruit of those in the grave by writing, "But Christ has indeed been raised from the dead, the first fruits of those who have fallen asleep."

Furthering this prophecy, Leviticus describes the Day of Atonement, which foreshadows the Jewish people's repentance during the second coming of Jesus. It is on that day they will receive him as their Messiah and be forgiven of all their sins. Leviticus 16:15–16 talks about the sacrifice of atonement, saying, "Then he shall kill the goat of the sin offering that is for the people and bring its blood inside the veil and do with its blood as he did with the blood of the bull, sprinkling it over the mercy seat and in front of the mercy seat. Thus he shalt make atonement for the Holy Place, because of the uncleanliness of the people of Israel and because of their transgressions, all their sins." Because of sacrifice, their sins were forgiven. The New Testament is full of verses that complete the message of atonement written in the Old Testament. In Rom 5:8, the apostle Paul expanded this idea. "But God demonstrates his own love for us in this: While we were still sinners, Christ died for us." The disciple Peter in 1 Pet 3:18 states, "For Christ also suffered once for sins, the righteous for the unrighteous, to bring you to God." Paul wrote his letter to believers in the region of Galatia, also known as Asia Minor. He wrote that Jesus, the Christ, is the One "who gave Himself for our sins so that He might rescue us from this present evil age, according to the will of our God and Father" (Gal 1:4). Jesus gave himself for our sins; he paid the penalty and provided atonement. From the beginning, people believed that God would rescue them from death, or at least they hoped so. King David knew without a doubt that God would rescue him from death He believed that there was a life after death with his God. And, because he always atoned for the sins he committed, he believed. In Ps 49:15 David believed, "But God will redeem me from the realm of the dead; he will surely take me to himself." Isaiah actually prophesied the resurrection of the Messiah in chapter 5, verse 8, when he said, "He will swallow up death forever. The Sovereign Lord will wipe away the tears from all faces; he will remove his people's disgrace from all the earth. The Lord has spoken."

How, then, do we know for sure that Jesus atoned for our sins, and why did he do it? The Israelites, living before Jesus, had to offer a sacrifice to atone for their sins. Exodus 12:3–6 describes the law concerning the Passover. When offering a sacrifice for the forgiveness of sins, the priests said, "Your lamb shall be without blemish, a male of the first year: ye shall take it out from the sheep" (Exod 12:5). Remember, John the Baptist saw Jesus and shouted, "Look, the Lamb of God, who takes away the sin of the world! This is the one I meant when I said, 'A man who comes after me has surpassed me because he was before me.' I myself did not know him, but the reason I came baptizing with water was that he might be revealed to Israel" (John 1:29–31). Jesus, this Lamb, was also without blemish. He was led to his death even though he was an innocent man. God allowed this to happen because he loved mankind so much, but only the act of the selfless sacrifice of blood would pay the price for our sins. Paul, when writing Rom 3:25, explained how God gave his Son and how he allowed him to die: "God presented Christ as a sacrifice of atonement, through the shedding of his blood—to be received by faith. He did this to demonstrate his righteousness, because in his forbearance he had left the sins committed beforehand unpunished."

The Old Testament in Isa 53:7 foretells, "He was led like a lamb to the slaughter." Moses wrote that "God himself will provide the lamb for the burnt offering," and, in Isa 53:4–5, the prophet mentioned the suffering servant: "Surely he took up our pain and bore our suffering, yet we considered him punished by God, stricken by him, and afflicted. But he was pierced for our transgressions, he was crushed for our iniquities; the punishment that brought us peace was on him, and by his wounds we are healed." The prophecy is so compelling that part of Isaiah's prophecy (in Isa 53:4–5) was quoted directly by Peter when talking about Jesus' death on the cross. "'He himself bore our sins' in his body on the cross, so that we might die to sins and live for righteousness; by his wounds you have been healed" (1 Pet 2:24).

Because of what Jesus did, we can accept the fact that his death was a sacrifice. Why, though, would God do this? The reason is twofold. First, God was showing his fairness and equal justice. In the past, God has forgiven his people over and over again. When Moses presented the law to the people of Israel, he taught them to follow it. If they failed and asked for forgiveness, God was quick to forgive. Jeremiah told the Jews that God had said, "No longer will they teach their neighbor, or say to one another, 'Know the Lord,' because they will all know me, from the least of them to the greatest," declares the Lord. "For I will forgive their wickedness and will remember their sins no more" (Jer 31:34). When they rebelled against the Lord again, Jer 33:8 told them, "I will cleanse them from all the sin they have committed against me and will forgive all their sins of rebellion against me." Even David expressed this forgiveness in the song of Ps 103:12: "As far as the east is from the west, so far has he removed our transgressions from us."

The second reason God forgives was shown in his love and willingness to accept the sinner, as his children, because the sinner had been cleansed by the blood sacrifice of Jesus. Jesus wanted to once again reconnect everyone with God. Because of this, the New Testament teaches that people are now justified in the eyes of God when they believe that Jesus sacrificed his life and shed his blood for them and when they accept him as their Lord and Savior. Their sins have been taken away. All they need do is accept Jesus.

It all began at the Last Supper; it was the final Passover that Jesus would see before his death. Anyone who has been to church would remember what he said at that table. Luke 22:17–20 described it. "After taking the cup, He gave thanks and said, 'Take this and divide it among you. For I tell you I will not drink again from the fruit of the vine until the kingdom of God comes.' And He took bread, gave thanks and broke it, and gave it to them, saying, 'This is my body given for you; do this in remembrance of me.' In the same way, after the supper he took the cup, saying, 'This cup is the new covenant in my blood, which is poured out for you.'"

Jesus sacrificed himself for the will of his Father in heaven. It was all a part of God's plan to restore mankind to himself. The reason Jesus came was to be a servant. "For even the Son of Man did not come to be served, but to serve, and to give his life as a ransom for many" (Mark 10:45). In 1 Pet 3:18, the disciple wrote, "For Christ also hath once suffered for sins, the just for the unjust, that he might bring us to God, being put to death in the flesh, but quickened by the Spirit." Jesus conquered sin and death, once and for all. Paul also told us that Jesus died on our behalf. John 3:16 says it all. "For God so loved the world that he gave his one and only Son, that whoever believes in him shall not perish but have eternal life." What do we do with this? Well, our Christ commanded us to "seek ye first the kingdom of God, and his righteousness" (Matt 6:33). Our willingness to be like him shows our love to God. For this is how we know what love is, and this is why we should live our lives like Jesus did. John said in 1 John 3:16, "This is how we know what love is: Jesus Christ laid down his life for us. And we ought to lay down our lives for our brothers and sisters."

Chapter 10

JESUS DEFINED AS GOD

THE RESURRECTED AND ASCENDED Lord is the basis for our salvation and the cornerstone of our beliefs. Jesus was rejected by many of his own people during his life. His own family members, some of his followers, and many political and religious Jews rejected him. Mark 6 explains how his own family treated him. "They asked, 'Where did he get all this wisdom and the power to perform such miracles?' Then they scoffed, 'He's just a carpenter, the son of Mary and the brother of James, Joseph, Judas, and Simon. And his sisters live right here among us.' They were deeply offended and refused to believe in him" (Mark 6:2–3). Family were not the only people to reject Jesus. His follower Peter, at one point, rejected Jesus and denied that he even knew him. Finally, the leaders of the Jewish people rejected him. When Jesus was casting out demons, the people asked if this man could be the Son of David. Matthew 12:24 expresses:

> When the Pharisees heard this, they said, "It is only by Beelzebub, the prince of demons, that this fellow drives out demons." Jesus knew their thoughts and said to them, "Every kingdom divided against itself will be ruined, and every city or household divided against itself will not stand. If Satan drives out Satan, he is divided against himself. How then can his kingdom stand? And if I drive out demons by Beelzebub, by whom do your people drive them out? So then, they will be your judges. But if it is by the Spirit of God that I drive out demons, then the kingdom of God has come upon you."

Jesus told the parable of the vineyard owner and at the end repeated a psalm of David. In Matt 21:42, Jesus said to them, "Have you never read in the Scriptures: The stone the builders rejected has become the cornerstone; the Lord has done this, and it is marvelous in our eyes"? He was referring to Ps 118:22–23: "The stone the builders rejected has become the cornerstone; the Lord has done this, and it is marvelous in our eyes." The same words are used in the Old Testament and the New.

Those who did not believe in the Messiah soon were outnumbered by believers. Isaiah, one of the most significant prophets from the Old Testament, repeated what the Lord told him to say. God told him to prophesy that the Jews were not the only people who would accept the Savior. Gentiles, like some of the Jews, would believe that Jesus was indeed the Lord. "In that day the Root of Jesse will stand as a banner for the peoples; the nations will rally to him, and his resting place will be glorious" (Isa 11:10). The nations of the world were to be included as those who believed. Isaiah 42:1 tells us, "Here is my servant whom I uphold, my chosen one in whom I delight; I will put my Spirit on him, and he will bring justice to the nations."

His prophecy concerning all nations was written about by many disciples and apostles. Mark, in chapter 27, verses 24 through 26, discussed those who came to Jesus. "Jesus left that place and went to the vicinity of Tyre. He entered a house and did not want anyone to know it; yet he could not keep his presence secret. In fact, as soon as she heard about him, a woman whose little daughter was possessed by an impure spirit came and fell at his feet. The woman was a Greek, born in Syrian Phoenicia. She begged Jesus to drive the demon out of her daughter." He did, and she believed. In Acts 13:48, Paul, formerly known as Saul, told everyone the good news about the Son of God. "When the Gentiles heard this, they were glad and honored the word of the Lord; and all who were appointed for eternal life believed."

The Old Testament told about the people of Israel and how they lived and what laws they were to follow. This was the first covenant between God and his chosen people. The old was established while Moses was on Mount Sinai, after the Jewish people were freed from Egyptian slavery. Around 1400 BC the law was given to Moses. That law contained Ten Commandments and, by the way, over six hundred more laws the Israelites were to follow. They were to keep the law, obey the law, and give sacrifices to atone for their sins. The Ten Commandments are well known and used to be presented in some public areas, such as schools and government buildings.

Sadly today, however, finding these commandments in public is rare. It is important to know what the hand of God gave to Moses. Exodus 20:1-2 explains, "And God spoke all of these words. 'I am the Lord your God, who brought you out of Egypt, out of the land of slavery.'"

THE TEN COMMANDMENTS

I	Thou shalt have no other gods before me
II	Thou shalt not make unto thee any graven image
III	Thou shalt not take the name of the Lord thy God in vain
IV	Remember the Sabbath day, to keep it holy
V	Honor thy father and thy mother
VI	Thou shalt not murder
VII	Thou shalt not commit adultery
VIII	Thou shalt not steal
IX	Thou shall not bear false witness against your neighbor
X	Thou shall not covet your neighbor's house. Thou shall not covet your neighbor's wife or anything that belongs to your neighbor. (Exod 20:3-17)

In the New Testament, however, Jesus gave a new commandment. It simplifies the old but covers all the laws that had previously been recorded. The New Testament provided a new covenant, which Jesus discussed to all he met. Although this isn't exactly a prophecy, it does show who had the power to simplify the law and share it with the world. Genesis 17:7 stated, "I will establish my covenant as an everlasting covenant between me and you and your descendants after you for the generations to come, to be your God and the God of your descendants after you." The disciple John, in John 13:34-35, explained this new covenant. It appears in his Gospel and says, "A new commandment I give unto you, That ye love one another; as I have loved you, that ye also love one another. By this shall all men know that ye are my disciples, if ye have love one to another."

There was a prophecy, though, that was fulfilled when Jesus spoke. Jeremiah, in chapter 31:31-34, says, "'The day is coming,' says the LORD, 'when I will make a new covenant with the people of Israel and Judah. This covenant will not be like the one I made with their ancestors when I took them by the hand and brought them out of the land of Egypt.'" Jesus fulfilled this prophecy and it was recorded by Matthew. The Sadducees and the Pharisees hated Jesus and were trying to trick him into saying something they could convict him on. "Teacher, which is the greatest commandment in the Law?" Jesus replied: "'Love the Lord your God with all your heart and with all your soul and with all your mind.' This is the first and greatest commandment. And the second is like it: 'Love your neighbor as yourself.' All the Law and the Prophets hang on these two commandments" (Matt 22:36–40).

The teacher of love and the fulfiller of the words of the prophets was the Messiah. This Son of Man was compared to God and actually was God. Isaiah called him, in a prophecy, Yahweh and Elohim. The Hebrew meaning Yahweh translates as "The Lord," and this implies that he is self-existing. Elohim describes that God has a relationship with his people and he is the ultimate power. He is the one who was, is, and will always be. He is the creator.

Isaiah claimed that Jesus would be the creator and also the God eternal. In John 1:1–5 the disciple said, "In the beginning was the Word, and the Word was with God, and the Word was God. He was with God in the beginning. Through him all things were made; without him nothing was made that has been made. In him was life, and that life was the light of all mankind. The light shines in the darkness, and the darkness has not overcome it." John called Jesus the Word. In Greek "the Word" is *Logos* (the Word of God, or principle of divine reason and creative order). The disciple explains to us in John 1 that Jesus was like his Heavenly Father. Jesus with God and as God was in the beginning before creation. Jesus was a deity, the creator, and supreme being. He was God and he was with God. He is the persona of God in the flesh. In Exod 3:14 God told Moses, "I am that I am"; John 10:25–30 claimed that Jesus and God were one and Jesus, too, claimed this. In John 8:58 Jesus said, "Before Abraham was born, I am!" Jesus was and is the Word, the living Word of God.

Paul called the Christ the image of God. In his letter to the Corinthians, he said that "the god of this age has blinded the minds of unbelievers, so that they cannot see the light of the gospel that displays the glory of Christ, who is the image of God" (2 Cor 4:4). Jesus said, "The works I do in my Father's name testify about me, but you do not believe because you are not my sheep. My sheep listen to my voice; I know them, and they follow me. I give them eternal life, and they shall never perish; no one will snatch them out of my hand. My Father, who has given them to me, is greater than all. I and the Father are one" (John 10:25–30). Isaiah's prophecy showed this image of Jesus as a shepherd. "Behold, the Lord God will come with strong hand, and his arm shall rule for him: behold, his reward is with him, and his work before him. He shall feed his flock like a shepherd: he shall gather the lambs with his arm, and carry them in his bosom, and shall gently lead those that are with young" (Isa 40:10–11). Isaiah was mirrored by the words of John, who wrote:

> I am the good shepherd; I know my sheep and my sheep know me—just as the Father knows me and I know the Father—and I lay down my life for my sheep. I have other sheep that are not of this sheep pen. I must bring them also. They too will listen to my voice, and there shall be one flock and one shepherd. The reason my Father loves me is that I lay down my life—only to take it up again. No one takes it from me, but I lay it down of my own accord. I have authority to lay it down and authority to take it up again. This command I received from my Father. (John 10:11–18)

As a good shepherd, Jesus gave his life for his sheep of his own free will.

Isaiah 40:3 also refers to the good shepherd as the way to receive redemption. He says, "A voice of one calling: In the wilderness prepare the way for the Lord; make straight in the desert a highway for our God." The voice is deemed to be that of God explaining how he was going to send a deliverer who would save Israel. In the New Testament, John the Baptist was preaching and telling God's people to repent. The Jewish leaders demanded that John tell them who he really was. In the Gospel of John 1:22–23, John wrote, "Finally they said, 'Who are you? Give us an answer to take back to those who sent us. What do you say about yourself?'" John replied in the words of Isaiah the prophet, "I am the voice of one calling in the desert, 'Make straight the way for the Lord.'"

Isaiah, in Isa 9:6, describes who God was and who the Messiah would be. He starts by claiming, "In the past He humbled the land of Zebulun and the land of Naphtali, but in the future he will honor Galilee of the nations, by the Way of the Sea, beyond the Jordan." Isaiah called the Messiah "Mighty God, Everlasting Father, Prince of Peace. For to us a child is born, to us a son is given, and the government will be on his shoulders. And he will be called Wonderful Counselor, Mighty God, Everlasting Father, Prince of Peace."

In verse 7 he explained who Jesus was to be and what he was to do. "Of the greatness of his government and peace there will be no end. He will reign on David's throne and over his kingdom, establishing and upholding it with justice and righteousness from that time on and forever. The zeal of the Lord Almighty will accomplish this."

The New Testament follows the words of Isaiah. Jesus is the Messiah. He claimed it in Mark 14:61–62. The leaders of the temple were questioning Jesus to find a way to have him killed. They asked if he thought he was the Son of God. "But Jesus remained silent and gave no answer. Again the high priest asked him, 'Are you the Messiah, the Son of the Blessed One?' 'I am,' said Jesus. 'And you will see the Son of Man sitting at the right hand of the Mighty One and coming on the clouds of heaven.'"

Jesus was the Messiah and also the Prince of Peace. The term comes from the Hebrew *Shar Shalom*, which means "the one who removes all peace-disturbing factors and secures the peace." He brought peace to be found within his followers, he asked us to seek peace with others in this world, and he gave us a chance for eternal peace with God. He offered this to all the people in the world, but it was to be their choice. He didn't come to conquer the world like human rulers and kings; he came to die for our sins and be the blood sacrifice for sin.

Jesus died for you and me, and all we need to believe is that he is the Messiah. He was at the beginning, he came to earth, and he died and was resurrected, and he returned to heaven to sit at the right hand of God and, surprisingly, he takes captives (sinners) with him, according to both Testaments. This was the case. David wrote in Ps 68:18 that "when you ascended on high, you took many captives; you received gifts from people, even from the rebellious—that you, Lord God, might dwell there." David describes Yahweh as a conquering king who ascended into heaven. Luke, on the other hand, describes Jesus as a conquering King who defeats death. In Luke 23:43 Jesus told the criminal that "truly I tell you, today you will be with me in paradise." The criminal who asked Jesus to remember him when he entered his heavenly kingdom was not the only one who would see Jesus sitting on his throne. The twelve disciples, not Judas, will be there. Matthew 19:28 describes a moment when Jesus will sit on his throne in heaven and his disciples will sit on twelve thrones with him. All Christians will see Jesus in heaven.

In Matthew's verses, in chapter 19, Jesus used the original word *palingenesia*, which means "spiritual rebirth," or more precisely, "people are born again and regenerated." Jesus made all of his believers a promise. He said, "I am the resurrection and the life. He who believes in Me, though he may die, he shall live" (John 11:25). Jesus, in John 14:2–6, also said, "'In My Father's house are many mansions; if it were not so, I would have told you. I go to prepare a place for you. And if I go and prepare a place for you, I will come again and receive you to Myself; that where I am, there you may be also. And where I go you know, and the way you know.' Thomas said to Him, 'Lord, we do not know where You are going, and how can we know the way?' Jesus said to him, 'I am the way, the truth, and the life. No one comes to the Father except through Me.'"

The Old Testament said it this way. Second Samuel 7:12–13 told us, "When your days are over and you rest with your ancestors, I will raise up your offspring to succeed you, your own flesh and blood, and I will establish his kingdom. He is the one who will build a house for my Name, and I will establish the throne of His kingdom forever." The kingdom of God and the throne of Jesus will last forever. The kingdom of God will eventually be heaven on earth. Psalm 6:10 states, "Be still and know that I am God; I will be exalted among the nations, I will be exalted over the earth." This will be realized through Jesus, who lived, died, and lived again. In Phil 2:11–12 we find out how the Messiah will be exalted among all nations. It says "that at the name of Jesus every knee should bow, of those in heaven, and of those on earth, and of those under the earth, and that every tongue should confess that Jesus Christ is Lord, to the glory of God the Father."

However, his literal reign hasn't even begun yet. We were promised that Jesus would return one day. In Rev 1:7 John said, "Behold, he cometh with clouds; and every eye shall see him, and they also which pierced him: and all kindred of the earth shall wail because of him. Even so, Amen." Jesus is coming again and it may not be too long.

Chapter 11

HE IS COMING AGAIN

JESUS, FROM HIS HEAVENLY THRONE, will be coming back to proclaim his right as the King. The book of Revelation, by John the apostle, gives us a glimpse of our own future; it's a future where we are given a choice. In his book, John explains, in detail, the final return of Jesus and the defeat of Satan. Just before that time, the devil will persecute true Christians, but they have to stand with the Lord even though their lives are threatened. They, however, will be protected and spiritually exonerated when the Messiah returns in the clouds. The evil one, himself, will be cast into hell and chained for a thousand years. The wicked will be destroyed, and God's believers will enter into the glorious presence of the Lord.

When, then, will all of this occur? Even the disciples of Jesus asked him when the end times would happen. The best answer can be found in the words of Jesus, himself. Matthew 24 explains and is the beginning of understanding the reason for the Revelation of John.

MATTHEW 24

Jesus left the temple and was going away, when his disciples came to point out to him the buildings of the temple. But he answered them, "You see all these, do you not? Truly, I say to you, there will not be left here one stone upon another that will not be thrown down." As he sat on the Mount of Olives, the disciples came to him privately, saying, "Tell us, when will these things be, and what will be the sign of your coming and of the end of the age?" And

Jesus answered them, "See that no one leads you astray. For many will come in my name, saying, 'I am the Christ,' and they will lead many astray. And you will hear of wars and rumors of wars. See that you are not alarmed, for this must take place, but the end is not yet. For nation will rise against nation, and kingdom against kingdom, and there will be famines and earthquakes in various places. All these are but the beginning of the birth pains.

"Then they will deliver you up to tribulation and put you to death, and you will be hated by all nations for my name's sake. And then many will fall away and betray one another and hate one another. And many false prophets will arise and lead many astray. And because lawlessness will be increased, the love of many will grow cold. But the one who endures to the end will be saved. And this gospel of the kingdom will be proclaimed throughout the whole world as a testimony to all nations, and then the end will come.

"So when you see the abomination of desolation spoken of by the prophet Daniel, standing in the holy place (let the reader understand), then let those who are in Judea flee to the mountains. Let the one who is on the housetop not go down to take what is in his house, and let the one who is in the field not turn back to take his cloak. And alas for women who are pregnant and for those who are nursing infants in those days! Pray that your flight may not be in winter or on a Sabbath. For then there will be great tribulation, such as has not been from the beginning of the world until now, no, and never will be. And if those days had not been cut short, no human being would be saved. But for the sake of the elect those days will be cut short. Then if anyone says to you, 'Look, there is the Christ!' or 'There he is!' do not believe it. For false Christs and false prophets will arise and perform great signs and wonders, so as to lead astray, if possible, even the elect. See, I have told you beforehand. So, if they say to you, 'Look, he is in the wilderness,' do not go out. If they say, 'Look, he is in the inner rooms,' do not believe it. For as the lightning comes from the east and shines as far as the west, so will be the coming of the Son of Man. Wherever the corpse is, there the vultures will gather.

"Immediately after the tribulation of those days the sun will be darkened, and the moon will not give its light, and the stars will fall from heaven, and the powers of the heavens will be shaken. Then will appear in heaven the sign of the Son of Man, and then all the tribes of the earth will mourn, and they will see the Son of Man coming on the clouds of heaven with power and great glory. And he will send out his angels with a loud trumpet call, and they will gather his elect from the four winds, from one end of heaven to the other.

"From the fig tree learn its lesson: as soon as its branch becomes tender and puts out its leaves, you know that summer is near. So also, when you see all these things, you know that he is near, at the very gates. Truly, I say to you, this generation will not pass away until all these things take place. Heaven and earth will pass away, but my words will not pass away.

"But concerning that day and hour no one knows, not even the angels of heaven, nor the Son, but the Father only. For as were the days of Noah, so will be the coming of the Son of Man. For as in those days before the flood they were eating and drinking, marrying and giving in marriage, until the day when Noah entered the ark, and they were unaware until the flood came and swept them all away, so will be the coming of the Son of Man. Then two men will be in the field; one will be taken and one left. Two women will be grinding at the mill; one will be taken and one left. Therefore, stay awake, for you do not know on what day your Lord is coming. But know this, that if the master of the house had known in what part of the night the thief was coming, he would have stayed awake and would not have let his house be broken into. Therefore you also must be ready, for the Son of Man is coming at an hour you do not expect."

The second coming will be unannounced! Although this is described in detail by John's Revelation, it is also prophesied throughout the entire Bible. There is only one who really knows what will happen and that, of course, is God. Matthew said, "No one knows when that day or hour will come. Even the angels in heaven and the Son don't know. Only the Father knows" (Matt 26:36). God has always known because he is the past, the present, and the future. He is outside of time, which is a concept we really know little to nothing about. Isaiah prophesied the word of God when he said, "Remember the former things of old, for I am God, and there is no other; I am God, and there is none like Me, declaring the end from the beginning, and from ancient times things that are not yet done, saying, 'My counsel shall stand, and I will do all My pleasure'" (Isa 46:9–10). The future is in his hands including the end times, or the time when Jesus will first return for his children and then, later, come to earth as a victorious King.

Not everyone agrees with the timeline of the coming end times age, especially the rapture. The two events, the rapture and the second coming of Jesus, may happen in succession. The rapture happens when the dead and living believers are caught up in the clouds with Jesus to return with him to heaven. The second coming is when Jesus comes back to earth to establish his kingdom. Although the word "rapture" is not recorded in the Bible, there are references to this event. Many have considered the Revelation of John a book of symbolic messages, but I believe that the prophecy will occur and that we may, indeed, be close to the return of Jesus, the Christ. The Lord Jesus told us of his return to gather together his believers. Paul wrote about the Messiah gathering his flock together. "For the Lord himself shall descend from heaven with a shout, with the voice of the archangel, and with the trump of God: and the dead in Christ shall rise first: Then we which are alive and remain shall be caught up together with them in the clouds, to meet the Lord in the air: and so shall we ever be with the Lord" (1 Thess 4:16–17).

The rapture and the second coming will occur at two separate times because, as I believe, they are two separate events. The "taking away" of the people who have died believing in Jesus and those Christians who are still alive will occur in the twinkling of an eye. The apostle Paul wrote in 1 Cor 15:52, "In a moment, in the twinkling of an eye, at the last trump: for the trumpet shall sound, and the dead shall be raised incorruptible, and we shall be changed." When Jesus first comes for his church, I believe that not everyone will see him. The scripture doesn't specify whether all people will see Jesus when the rapture happens. That time will certainly be confusing. Those who did not accept Jesus as Lord and Savior will not disappear, but many will change their mind after the event happens. They will turn to Christianity and believe but will remain on earth throughout the tribulation. They will be hunted and some will be killed by the antichrist and his anti-Christian armies.

During the second coming of Jesus, there will be a totally different outcome. In Rev 1:7 the Bible describes the second coming. It explains that "every eye will see Him." Everyone in the whole world will see his return. This will begin the final battle between God and Satan—good and evil. This battle will save God's people, the Jewish nation, from total annihilation. It is, in fact, the last of the Jewish nation, redeemed by Jesus, who had accepted the Messiah and spread the message of the gospel during the tribulation. These Jews are "the hundred and forty-four thousand, which were redeemed from the earth" mentioned in Rev 14:3. Jesus was, indeed, the Messiah and they finally embrace him. The Old Testament records what will happen. "And I will pour out on the house of David and the inhabitants of Jerusalem a spirit of grace and pleas for mercy, so that, when they look on me, on him whom they have pierced, they shall mourn for him, as one mourns for an only child, and weep bitterly over him, as one weeps over a firstborn" (Zech 12:10). When Jesus and his army of angels and saints touch earth again, it will happen on the same ground where he ascended. Acts 1:12 states that Jesus will return "in like manner as you saw him go into heaven." Zechariah 14:4 also tell us Jesus' feet will be standing on the Mount of Olives. "East of Jerusalem, and the Mount of Olives will be split in two from east to west, forming a great valley, with half of the mountain moving north and half moving south."

Satan will lose and be thrown into the abyss, and Jesus will set up his kingdom. "I saw thrones on which were seated those who had been given authority to judge. And I saw the souls of those who had been beheaded because of their testimony about Jesus and because of the word of God. They had not worshiped the beast or its image and had not received its mark on their foreheads or their hands. They came to life and reigned with Christ a thousand years" (Rev 1:4). When Jesus comes again, he will judge the nations and will divide the righteous from the wicked (Matt 25:31–46).

Chapter 12

"COME UP HERE"

THIS REVELATION, AS WELL as other warnings, were given to John while he was a captive of Domitian, the Roman emperor, beginning in AD 81. He had been placed in exile on the island of Patmos, off of the coast of Roman-controlled Asia. He was there because of his Christian views. While he was there he received his visions. He listened to Jesus and began his book. The first five chapters the book of Revelation are actually in chronological order. The middle chapters are based on themes, and the last four are again recorded chronologically. The entire book is, itself, a prophecy of things yet to come.

The book begins with John receiving a vision. He is guided by the Spirit and sees Jesus, in all his glory among the church, giving instruction, encouragement, and orders to the seven churches of Asia Minor found in the end times. He asks the saints to pay attention, for these seven churches are the reflected light from the Christ shining to the rest of the world. Giving credit where credit is due, John begins, "The revelation from Jesus Christ, which God gave him to show his servants what must soon take place. He made it known by sending his angel to his servant John, who testifies to everything he saw—that is, the word of God and the testimony of Jesus Christ" (Rev 1:1–2). Since the Revelation was actually prophesied in the book of Daniel, in the Old Testament, as well as references found in Isaiah, Ezekiel, Zechariah, Joel, Amos, and Malachi, it becomes a bit more than a coincidence. What John said and recorded was a reflection of that prophecy. After telling of the angel's visit, John sees the worship of the Almighty God sitting on his throne. God is holding, in his right hand, a scroll containing seven seals. Isaiah 56:1 explains why the angels in heaven are worshiping Jesus. The prophet proclaimed, "Thus says the Lord: Keep justice, and do righteousness, for soon my salvation will come, and my righteousness be revealed."

The church of Jesus (the believers) is called to live holy lives until the conquering Lord comes again. Salvation will happen when the anointed King of kings returns. Isaiah 61:6 gives us a message of the fulfillment of the promises Jesus gave. "The Spirit of the Lord God is upon me, because the Lord has anointed me to bring good news to the poor; he has sent me to bind up the brokenhearted, to proclaim liberty to the captives, and the opening of the prison to those who are bound; to proclaim the year of the Lord's favor, and the day of vengeance of our God; to comfort all who mourn. The day of God's vengeance is close at hand."

John sees the Christ, now, as a resurrected Lord, as an older, wiser, Savior, who will also judge all of mankind. Hebrews 4:13 explains Jesus this way, "Nothing in all creation is hidden from God's sight. Everything is uncovered and laid bare before the eyes of him to whom we must give account." The prophecy of Isaiah, in Isa 11:4, explains the Messiah as a judge by writing, "with righteousness shall he judge the poor, and reprove with equity for the meek of the earth: and he shall smite the earth with the rod of his mouth, and with the breath of his lips shall he slay the wicked." His message then, to the seven churches, is of the judgment about to come to the enemies of God and the hope that is given to true believers.

Jesus showed John what would happen next. He told John to "come up here" so that the Christ could show him the future. This "coming up" mirrors what will happen when Jesus calls his followers to himself. Today we call it the rapture. Even though the word "rapture" is not used in the Bible, it is referred to. The Greek word *harpazo* is the origin of the English word "rapture," meaning to seize upon, spoil, snatch away, or take to oneself. It may also come from the Latin word *raptus*, which means "seized" or "carried away." It is with these words that John refers to this rapture of the church. He states, "After this I looked, and there before me was a door standing open in heaven. And the voice I had first heard speaking to me like a trumpet said, 'Come up here, and I will show you what must take place after this'" (Rev 4:1). In 1 Thess 4:14–18, the apostle Paul wrote about this coming up, too. He said, "The Lord will descend from heaven, a trumpet call will sound, and the dead in Christ will rise first" (1 Thess 4:16). Then, "we who are still alive and are left will be caught up [*harpazo* or *raptus*] together with them in the clouds to meet the Lord in the air" (1 Thess 4:17). At this point, all believers will receive new, incorruptible bodies as they enter eternity.

In the Old Testament, Isa 24:3 makes reference to "the land shall be utterly emptied, and utterly spoiled: for the Lord hath spoken this word." Here the empty land may describe what follows the rapture by an utterly spoiled world during the tribulation. Daniel is a bit more precise. In Dan 12:1–2 he wrote, "At that time Michael, the great prince who protects your people, will arise. There will be a time of distress such as has not happened from the beginning of nations until then. But at that time your people—everyone whose name is found written in the book—will be delivered. Multitudes who sleep in the dust of the earth will awake: some to everlasting life, others to shame and everlasting contempt."

After the believers have been taken up into the clouds to be with Jesus, chaos will begin. Just imagine standing next to someone you may know and, in a blink of an eye, they are taken. Jesus told us what would cause all the chaos. He was prophesying what would happen at the end of the age. He said in Matt 24:34–44:

> Truly I tell you, this generation will certainly not pass away until all these things have happened. Heaven and earth will pass away, but my words will never pass away. But about that day or hour no one knows, not even the angels in heaven, nor the Son, but only the Father. As it was in the days of Noah, so it will be at the coming of the Son of Man. For in the days before the flood, people were eating and drinking, marrying and giving in marriage, up to the day Noah entered the ark; and they knew nothing about what would happen until the flood came and took them all away. That is how it will be at the coming of the Son of Man. Two men will be in the field; one will be taken and the other left. Two women will be grinding with a hand mill; one will be taken and the other left. Therefore keep watch, because you do not know on what day your Lord will come. But understand this: If the owner of the house had known at what time of night the thief was coming, he would have kept watch and would not have let his house be broken into. So you also must be ready, because the Son of Man will come at an hour when you do not expect him.

This will happen because the people of the earth will turn away from God as the people did in the time of Noah. We can all remember the story of Noah and the ark. During that time, "the Lord saw how great the wickedness of the human race had become on the earth, and that every inclination of the thoughts of the human heart was only evil all the time. The Lord regretted that he had made human beings on the earth, and his heart was deeply troubled" (Gen 6:5–6). The rapture will become fact when mankind has deleted Jesus from their lives to believe in themselves as their own gods. Paul wrote this in his letters to Timothy. We read in 1 Tim 3:1–7, "There will be terrible times in the last days. People will be lovers of themselves, lovers of money, boastful, proud, abusive, disobedient to their parents, ungrateful, unholy, without love, unforgiving, slanderous, without self-control, brutal, not lovers of the good, treacherous, rash, conceited, lovers of pleasure rather than lovers of God—having a form of godliness but denying its power."

When Jesus does return, non-believers who have rejected Jesus will be left in a confused world. There is, however, hope. You may have been a church member and heard the word of prophecy, but you never really believed Jesus would return. You may have read the Bible but simply considered it to be a good book. You could have thought you did good things and were good enough to go with God, but you never really accepted him.

Maybe you never believed the word of God before but now, after the rapture, you begin to listen. You may hear the two witnesses that will come, in the name of the Lord, to preach the word of redemption. You may listen to the 144,00 Jewish people who have turned to Jesus and now accept him as Messiah, preaching the gospel all over the world. They will be telling everyone that there is still time to come to Jesus before the final judgment. At that point, you may accept the Messiah. The times of trouble will soon come to you, but you know you must fight for your salvation. At first peace will come to the world. The leader of this peace will deceive the world but, after three and a half years, he will break that peace and declare war on Christians and Jews alike. These new Christians who stand fast to their new belief, accepted after the rapture, will be hunted during this time of hardship and suffering. They will remain loyal and steadfast in the Lord and will die for their faith. However, "they overcame [Satan] by the blood of the Lamb and by the word of their testimony; they did not love their lives so much as to shrink from death" (Rev 12:11).

They will be saved even unto death. "He who sits on the throne will spread his tent over them. Never again will they hunger; never again will they thirst. The sun will not beat upon them, nor any scorching heat. For the Lamb at the center of the throne will be their shepherd; he will lead them to springs of living water. And God will wipe away every tear from their eyes" (Rev 7:15–17).

Those left behind who do not accept the word will soon realize following the antichrist is no longer a choice. During this time of great trouble, the followers of evil will join in to oppress and harass the believer because of the antichrist's actions. Daniel saw the antichrist "engaging in war against the saints and defeating them" (Dan 7:21). These followers of Satan will be required to bow down to this evil ruler or choose death. They will accept him as their god so they will not end up as the martyred Christians. There is, however, much debate on when this rapture will take place. Some think it will occur at the beginning of the seven-year tribulation, some believe it will happen in the middle, while others are not sure at all. I, after researching Scripture, believe in the pre-tribulation rapture.

First of all, the judgment and rescue that brings us to "the day of the Lord" is found throughout the entire Bible and signifies a time of terrible judgment from God. David wrote gentle words to show the day God has in store for mankind. David sang, in 2 Sam 23:6 (NIV) "But evil men are all to be cast aside like thorns, which are not gathered with the hand."

The most descriptive one, however, I found in Zechariah. The prophet clarifies the second coming, where the saints are already in heaven. The rapture would have to already have occurred for the saints to return a final time with the Lord. "Thus the Lord my God will come, And all the saints with Him . . . . And the Lord shall be King over all the earth. In that day it shall be—The Lord is one, and His name one" (Zech 14:1–9).

The New Testament follows this idea. For example, Paul wrote, "For the mystery of lawlessness is already at work; only He who now restrains will do so until he is taken out of the way. And then the lawless one will be revealed, whom the Lord will consume with the breath of His mouth and destroy with the brightness of His coming" (2 Thess 2:3–8). Paul also states, "For you yourselves are fully aware that the day of the Lord will come like a thief in the night. While people are saying, 'There is peace and security,' then sudden destruction will come upon them as labor pains come upon a pregnant woman, and they will not escape" (1 Thess 5:2).

The Messiah knows how to save his believers. He knows that the antichrist will be bringing destruction to the earth. I believe he will take up his church before that devastation and that time of chaos. The disciple Peter wrote, "The Lord knows how to rescue the godly from trials, and to keep the unrighteous under punishment until the day of judgment" (2 Pet 2:9).

A pre-tribulation rapture, then, makes sense if Jesus is going to rescue the believers before the chaos of Satan.

Chapter 13

TRIBULATION AND
THE ANTICHRIST

I AM OF THE BELIEF that claims the rapture will happen before the rise of the antichrist. After the rapture a man will rise up as a peacemaker to the world. Joel A. Barker said, "The image of the beast, as described in the Book of Revelation, is a symbol of the end times, representing a powerful and manipulative force that deceives and controls people. In today's world, chatbots and other artificial intelligence programs are becoming increasingly prevalent and sophisticated, raising the question of whether they could potentially fulfill the prophecy of the image of the beast."[1] John wrote, "Here is wisdom. Let him that hath understanding count the number of the beast: for it is the number of a man; and his number is six hundred threescore and six" (Rev 13:18). This 666 is in total opposition and a mockery to the number 7. The number 7 is defined as completion and perfection; 777, then, would be associated with the Trinity: the Father, the Son, and the Holy Spirit. The Beast was thrown out of heaven because he rebelled against God.

Isaiah 14:12–15 describes why. "How you have fallen from heaven, morning star, son of the dawn! You have been cast down to the earth, you who once laid low the nations! You said in your heart, 'I will ascend to the heavens; I will raise my throne above the stars of God; I will sit enthroned on the mount of assembly, on the utmost heights of Mount Zaphon. I will

1. Barker, "ChatGPT, AI."

ascend above the tops of the clouds; I will make myself like the Most High.' But you are brought down to the realm of the dead, to the depths of the pit."

The New Testament defines Satan as the tempter, the ruler of demons, and the god of this world. Matthew tells the story of Jesus fasting in the desert for forty days preparing for his work on earth. During that time, Satan came to him and tempted him three times. In Matt 4:10, Jesus said to the devil, "Away from me, Satan. For it is written: 'Worship the Lord your God, and serve him only.'" Further, in chapter 12, Matthew refers to Satan as the ruler of the demons. Paul claims, in 2 Cor 4:4, that "the god of this age has blinded the minds of unbelievers, so that they cannot see the light of the gospel that displays the glory of Christ, who is the image of God." Jesus knew exactly who the devil was, because he had seen him before. Luke 10:18–19 explains: Jesus had sent seventy-two believers into all corners of the countryside. When they returned they were filled with joy, telling Jesus, "Lord, even the demons submit to us in your name." The Lord explained to them why this had happened. Jesus said, "I have observed Satan fall like lightning from the sky. Behold, I have given you the power 'to tread upon serpents' and scorpions and upon the full force of the enemy and nothing will harm you."

This beast, that Jesus saw, was also referred to as the antichrist and the beast from the abyss. The beast's image persecutes God's people, and its name is placed on the foreheads of its followers. First, Jesus established a time when Satan would take over the last days. Remember, Jesus told his disciples this event would occur when the fig tree bloomed. Matthew told the story. "'Now learn this parable from the fig tree: When its branch has already become tender and puts forth leaves, you know that summer is near. So you also, when you see all these things, know that it is near—at the doors! Assuredly, I say to you, this generation will by no means pass away till all these things take place. Heaven and earth will pass away, but My words will by no means pass away'" (Matt 24:32–35).

Ezekiel told the story of the dry bones in Ezek 37. The story began when God took Ezekiel to a certain valley. "The hand of the Lord was on me, and he brought me out by the Spirit of the Lord and set me in the middle of a valley; it was full of bones. He led me back and forth among them, and I saw a great many bones on the floor of the valley, bones that were very dry. He asked me, 'Son of man, can these bones live?'" The prophet told God that only he knew. God then asked Ezekiel to prophesy that the bones would live again. They came together, gained flesh, and began to breathe. Ezekiel then said:

> Then he said to me: "Son of man, these bones are the people of Israel. They say, 'Our bones are dried up and our hope is gone; we are cut off.' Therefore prophesy and say to them: 'This is what the Sovereign Lord says: My people, I am going to open your graves and bring you up from them; I will bring you back to the land of Israel. Then you, my people, will know that I am the Lord, when I open your graves and bring you up from them. I will put my Spirit in you and you will live, and I will settle you in your own land. Then you will know that I the Lord have spoken, and I have done it,' declares the Lord."

God kept his word. Israelites came from every corner of the world and settled in the promised land. At midnight on May 14, 1948, the provisional government of Israel proclaimed a new state of Israel. God had brought his people home. The generation that started the state of Israel has not passed away, but because of this act, the last days may be upon us.

Jesus also told his disciples that the end of days would be like the days of Noah. Even though this book is named after Saint Timothy, Paul wrote this epistle to Timothy, who was with him on his missions to preach the gospel. In 2 Tim 3:2–5 the last days are described. "But mark this: There will be terrible times in the last days. People will be lovers of themselves, lovers of money, boastful, proud, abusive, disobedient to their parents, ungrateful, unholy, without love, unforgiving, slanderous, without self-control, brutal, not lovers of the good, treacherous, rash, conceited, lovers of pleasure rather than lovers of God—having a form of godliness but denying its power. Have nothing to do with such people." First Thessalonians 5:3 also show what will happen. "Whenever it is that they are saying, 'Peace and security!' then sudden destruction is to be instantly on them, just like birth pains on a pregnant woman, and they will by no means escape." If we are, indeed, in the end times, we need to know what is about to happen.

Revelation 20:8–9 describes a gathering of nations for battle. "There are so many people they will be like sand on the seashore. And Satan's army marched across the earth and gathered around the camp of God's people and the city God loves." Isaiah and Zechariah both described the coming together of nations to attack the nation of Israel. "Listen, a noise on the mountains, like that of a great multitude! Listen, an uproar among the kingdoms, like nations massing together! The Lord Almighty is mustering an army for war. They come from faraway lands, from the ends of the heaven—the Lord and the weapons of his wrath—to destroy the whole country" (Isa 13:4–5).

How could this happen, when the person leading the people to war was the same one who, only three and one half years ago, signed a peace treaty with Israel and promised them seven years of peace? Daniel describes this time as an image of the world's obliteration. Nothing survives the rage of the antichrist. Daniel notes that a beast in his dream was different from all the beasts he had ever seen. This beast, or antichrist, is given "a period of seventy sets of seven has been decreed for your people and your holy city to finish their rebellion, to put an end to their sin, to atone for their guilt, to bring in everlasting righteousness, to confirm the prophetic vision, and to anoint the Most Holy Place" (Dan 9:24–27). John saw two beasts in his vision of the tribulation. The first beast was the antichrist, who was raised out of the sea. He was given the authority and breath by the second beast, which is referred to as the dragon. It is the image of this beast that persecutes God's people in the second part of Rev 13, and it is the name of this beast that is put on the foreheads of his followers (see Rev 13:16–17). The second beast is a monster that comes from the earth and is known as the false prophet. This beast forces all mankind to worship the antichrist and requires all to receive a mark on their forehead or right hand. Without the mark, people are unable to buy or sell anything. The mark refers to the first beast's name or number, which is 666.

Daniel 9:7 describe what the antichrist will do. He will bring about the abomination of desolation. "He will confirm a covenant with many for one 'seven.' In the middle of the 'seven' he will put an end to sacrifice and offering. And at the temple he will set up an abomination that causes desolation, until the end that is decreed is poured out on him." Matthew, as well as Mark 13, discussed this abomination. "But when you see the abomination of desolation standing where he ought not to be (let the reader understand), then let those who are in Judea flee to the mountains" (Mark 13:14). An abomination is something that causes disgust and, in the Old Testament, the word translated as "abomination" is *shiqquwts*, which comes from the Hebrew root *shaqats*, meaning "to be filthy." What the antichrist does in Israel is filth to God Almighty. When the antichrist, or Satan if you prefer, tries to take the place of God and requires he be worshiped as God, he has, unknowingly or not, brought on the kingdom of the Messiah and the Lamb of God.

Even the Jewish people of God will realize, after the antichrist has broken the peace treaty and is attempting to rid the world of them, that Jesus was and is the Messiah. His second coming will occur to deliver his people out of the hand of Satan. Zechariah 12:10 signifies this conversion. "And I will pour out on the house of David and the inhabitants of Jerusalem a spirit of grace and supplication. They will look on me, the one they have pierced, and they will mourn for him as one mourns for an only child, and grieve bitterly for him as one grieves for a firstborn son." In Rom 11:26 Paul explains how Jesus will turn his children away from the beliefs of old and change their understanding of the Messiah. Paul wrote, "And in this way all Israel will be saved. As it is written: 'The deliverer will come from Zion; he will turn godlessness away from Jacob.'"

Chapter 14

"WORTHY IS THE LAMB"

DURING THE TIME OF the tribulation, God prepares heaven for the attempted takeover of the world by Satan. Since Jesus is indeed God, he allowed his disciple John to view what was to happen on earth and in heaven during the last days. John wrote, "The revelation from Jesus Christ, which God gave him to show his servants what must soon take place. He made it known by sending his angel to his servant John" (Rev 1:1). While in the Spirit and having ascended to heaven, John saw a throne. Revelation 4:3–8 elaborates the vision.

> And the one who sat there had the appearance of jasper and ruby. A rainbow that shone like an emerald encircled the throne. Surrounding the throne were twenty-four other thrones, and seated on them were twenty-four elders. They were dressed in white and had crowns of gold on their heads. From the throne came flashes of lightning, rumblings and peals of thunder. In front of the throne, seven lamps were blazing. These are the seven spirits of God. Also in front of the throne there was what looked like a sea of glass, clear as crystal.
> In the center, around the throne, were four living creatures, and they were covered with eyes, in front and in back. The first living creature was like a lion, the second was like an ox, the third had a face like a man, the fourth was like a flying eagle. Each of the four living creatures had six wings and was covered with eyes all around, even under its wings. Day and night they never stop saying: "Holy, holy, holy is the Lord God Almighty, who was, and is,

and is to come." The one on the throne was the one who deserved all glory and praise.

What are these creatures that worship Jesus? The words in Revelation do not describe these creatures as symbolic. They are absolutely real angelic beings belonging to a special order of angels often referred to as cherubim. Ezekiel saw a vision of God and with him were the four creatures that John observed in Revelation. In Ezek 1:4–12 the prophet saw the same four creatures coming down as if in a fire. He wrote of the experience by stating:

> The center of the fire looked like glowing metal, and in the fire was what looked like four living creatures. In appearance their form was human, but each of them had four faces and four wings. Their legs were straight; their feet were like those of a calf and gleamed like burnished bronze. Under their wings on their four sides they had human hands. All four of them had faces and wings, and the wings of one touched the wings of another. Each one went straight ahead; they did not turn as they moved. Their faces looked like this: Each of the four had the face of a human being, and on the right side each had the face of a lion, and on the left the face of an ox; each also had the face of an eagle. Such were their faces. They each had two wings spreading out upward, each wing touching that of the creature on either side; and each had two other wings covering its body. Each one went straight ahead. Wherever the spirit would go, they would go, without turning as they went.

These cherubim had four faces: one a lion, one an ox, the third like a man, and the fourth an eagle. Although there are no exact definitions of these four angels, the Bible does make references to the animals. There are theologians who assert that the four are describing the tribes of Israel and God's love for them.

First, the lion is used as an example of Judah. Jacob was explaining the future to his sons and states, "You are a lion's cub, Judah; you return from the prey, my son. Like a lion he crouches and lies down, like a lioness—who dares to rouse him?" (Gen 49:9). He goes further in verse 10 and describes the Messiah who is to come. "The scepter will not depart from Judah, nor the ruler's staff from between his feet, until he to whom it belongs shall come and the obedience of the nations shall be his." Jesus, of course, was called the Lion of Judah. In Deuteronomy Ephraim, the grandson of Jacob and the son of Joseph, was a sign of Joseph's fruitfulness. Moses was blessing the tribes of Israel and when he blessed Joseph's decedents, including Ephraim through him, he said, "In majesty he is like a firstborn bull; his horns are the horns of a wild ox" (Deut 33:17). The image of the ox shows strength and influence. It is an animal who is used to make one fruitful. The name "Ephraim" comes from the Hebrew root *pārā*, which means "to be fruitful."

The third face on the four living creatures was that of a man. Genesis 29:32 told about Jacob and Leah, who had her first son, and they named him Reuben, which means "see, a son." Many scholars associate this with the face of a man described by John in Revelation. However, the popular symbolism for the third face of the creature is connected to Jesus, as the perfect man who was the savior of mankind.

Finally, the fourth face was that of an eagle. In Exodus and Deuteronomy, Moses showed the Jewish people God's relationship with all of the tribes. He reminded them of God's love. "You yourselves have seen what I did to Egypt, and how I carried you on eagles' wings and brought you to myself" (Exod 19:4). God gave the tribes of Israel the promised land and divided it among the twelve. Deuteronomy 32:6–11 also uses the eagle, inferring God's covenant and connection to Israel.

> When the Most High gave the nations their inheritance, when he divided all mankind, he set up boundaries for the peoples according to the number of the sons of Israel. For the Lord's portion is his people, Jacob his allotted inheritance. In a desert land he found him, in a barren and howling waste. He shielded him and cared for him; he guarded him as the apple of his eye, like an eagle that stirs up its nest and hovers over its young, that spreads its wings to catch them and carries them aloft.

As stated, some biblical scholars adhere to these comparisons. Others, however, have expressed that the four faces represent the four cardinal points on a compass. Tony Scialdone, for example, author of *GodWords: Theology and Other Stuff*, wrote about the four compass comparison, among other ideas about the four faces. He said that others were wondering about

the connections between these things found in Scripture:

- The cardinal points on a compass (North, South, East, West)
- The ancient Israelite tribes of Judah, Ephraim, Dan, and Reuben
- A lion, an eagle, an ox, and a man
- The gospels of Matthew, Mark, Luke, and John

It appears that most of this is traditional, rather than scriptural. That's not to say they're not well-established, though. For example:

a quick look at the history of Christian art shows that the writers of the gospels are often associated with those four animals. Small things found in the Bible, or interpreted from the Bible, seem to have led to these symbols being used. I wouldn't suggest that there's any deep, hidden spiritual meaning in these connections. If there were, it would be spelled out in the Bible for all to see.[1]

However, the four compass points were used by the tribes of Israel, who would arrange themselves around the tabernacle. In doing so, using the cardinal points of the compass, God would be the center of them all. Still other theologians would simply associate the four faces with the Gospels of Matthew, Mark, Luke, and John. Bible Hub, in "Symbolism of the Four Faces," uses this comparison:

> In the New Testament, the Apostle John echoes this imagery in his vision of the four living creatures around the throne of God. Revelation 4:7 states, "The first living creature was like a lion, the second was like an ox, the third had a face like a man, and the fourth was like a flying eagle." These creatures are often interpreted as representations of the four Gospels, each highlighting a different aspect of Christ's ministry:
>
> - Matthew: The lion, emphasizing Christ as the King and Messiah.
> - Mark: The ox, focusing on Christ as the Servant and Sacrifice.
> - Luke: The man, portraying Christ's humanity and compassion.
> - John: The eagle, illustrating Christ's divinity and heavenly origin.[2]

No matter the meaning and symbolism of the four faces described in the Revelation, the fact remains that the four living creatures have a purpose, and that purpose was to show that the worship they give Jesus is the same that would be bestowed to the Father. They are representatives of the Almighty and they call all to worship Jesus as the Messiah.

Revelation 4:11–14 continues with the worship of the one on the throne. "Whenever the living creatures give glory, honor, and thanks to him who sits on the throne and who lives for ever and ever, the twenty-four elders fall down before him who sits on the throne and worship him who lives for ever and ever. They lay their crowns before the throne and say: 'You are

---

1. Scialdone, "Ox, Man, Lion, Eagle."
2. Bible Hub, "Symbolism of the Four Faces."

worthy, our Lord and God, to receive glory and honor and power, for you created all things, and by your will they were created and have their being.'"

The one on the throne was described as the Lamb of God. Beside him, John saw a scroll with writing on both sides of it and containing seven seals. The angels and the elders were praising the One on the throne, while a mighty angel asked who was worthy to open the seals. John began to cry when he heard this, because no one was worthy. The elders comforted John and said there was one worthy, and he was the Lamb who had been sacrificed for the sins of the world. The Lamb then took the scrolls. Revelation 5:8–13 continues:

> And when he had taken it, the four living creatures and the twenty-four elders fell down before the Lamb. Each one had a harp and they were holding golden bowls full of incense, which are the prayers of God's people. And they sang a new song, saying: "You are worthy to take the scroll and to open its seals, because you were slain, and with your blood you purchased for God persons from every tribe and language and people and nation. You have made them to be a kingdom and priests to serve our God, and they will reign on the earth." Then I looked and heard the voice of many angels, numbering thousands upon thousands, and ten thousand times ten thousand. They encircled the throne and the living creatures and the elders. In a loud voice they were saying: "Worthy is the Lamb, who was slain, to receive power and wealth and wisdom and strength and honor and glory and praise!" Then I heard every creature in heaven and on earth and under the earth and on the sea, and all that is in them, saying: "To him who sits on the throne and to the Lamb be praise and honor and glory and power for ever and ever!"

This Lamb was prophesied by many through the Old Testament and the New Testament. It is interesting that God sent Jesus to be the sacrificial Lamb, and Genesis referred to this during the sacrifice of Isaac by his father, Abraham. God, testing Abraham, stopped the sacrifice and provided a lamb to take Isaac's place. This story actually foretells the gospel of Jesus, God's Son. When Isaac asked his father, Abraham, "Where is the lamb for the burnt offering?" Abraham responded, "God himself will provide the lamb for the burnt offering, my son" (Gen 22:7–8).

So, the one who was worthy to open the seals in Revelation, described in Genesis and seen by John on the throne in heaven, was the Messiah, the Christ, the Son of God. Remember, Jesus was the one referred to as the

Word in John's Gospel. John saw Jesus as God and described this in his book. "In the beginning was the Word, and the Word was with God, and the Word was God. He was with God in the beginning. Through him all things were made; without him nothing was made that has been made. In him was life, and that life was the light of all mankind. The light shines in the darkness, and the darkness has not overcome it" (John 1:1–5). Truly Jesus is the worthy Lamb.

This was the beginning of John's tribulation vision. In the Spirit, John saw the start of the seven-year tribulation. The prophet Jeremiah expressed the tribulation and called it the "time of Jacob's trouble," which he explained as the final attack on the children of Israel before the reign of God on earth. Daniel was much more precise when he wrote his prophecy found in Dan 9:24–27.

> Seventy weeks are decreed about your people and your holy city, to finish the transgression, to put an end to sin, and to atone for iniquity, to bring in everlasting righteousness, to seal both vision and prophet, and to anoint a most holy place. Know therefore and understand that from the going out of the word to restore and build Jerusalem to the coming of an anointed one, a prince, there shall be seven weeks. Then for sixty-two weeks it shall be built again with squares and moat, but in a troubled time. And after the sixty-two weeks, an anointed one shall be cut off and shall have nothing. And the people of the prince who is to come shall destroy the city and the sanctuary. Its end shall come with a flood, and to the end there shall be war. Desolations are decreed. And he shall make a strong covenant with many for one week, and for half of the week he shall put an end to sacrifice and offering. And on the wing of abominations shall come one who makes desolate, until the decreed end is poured out on the one who desolates.

The vision of John began with Jesus showing his servant John what must soon take place. Next, the horrors that await a sinful world are about to be realized.

John observed the Lamb of God holding a scroll in his hand, and Rev 6 showed him what would happen when the Lamb of God broke open the seals on the scroll. The seven seals are to be opened by Jesus in the last days, and this will be the beginning of the end, as it were, contained in Bible prophecy. Revelation describes this as a time of great tribulation, when many people will face death and destruction on earth because of catastrophic events. The four horsemen are represented by the first four seals that will be opened. They are described as riders on a white horse, a red horse, a black horse, and a pale horse. The white represents conquest and the rider has a bow and a crown, but he is not a deliverer. He is a deceiver, an antichrist. The red horse brings war and carries a great sword. The black horse will bring the world economic disaster, and the pale horse brings us death. They will be creating war, spreading pestilence, and causing famine. This is the time to repent, because God will be judging the earth for its sins. It is a time to believe God or follow a deceiver. All four riders will come in succession and will begin the reign of the antichrist who wants to assume total power over the entire world.

John was shown these first four seals, which represent the apocalypse. These four horsemen are not explicitly mentioned in the book of Daniel, but the Bible does include a visions of four beasts. Daniel 7 explains how there would be four kingdoms, with the last being controlled by the antichrist. Daniel 7:23 clarifies this. "Thus he said, The fourth beast shall be the fourth kingdom upon earth, which shall be diverse from all kingdoms, and shall devour the whole earth, and shall tread it down, and break it in pieces."

Instead of four kingdoms, Ezekiel elaborates on the four seals in chapter 14 verse 21 and explains the first four seals as God's judgment. The Lord identifies his four acts of judgment, sword, famine, wild beasts, and pestilence against the idolatrous people of Israel. Ezekiel used symbolism to show the four horsemen in Revelation and the judgments they would bring, and wrote, "For this is what the Sovereign Lord says: How much worse will it be when I send against Jerusalem my four dreadful judgments—sword and famine and wild beasts and plague—to kill its men and their animals!"

The remaining fifth, sixth, and seventh seals represent victims, killed during the times of persecution, earthquakes where mankind tries to hide from the devastation, and silence in heaven ending with the victorious return of Jesus. To understand the prophecy given in both the Old Testament and the New concerning these seven seals, a closer look at each is needed.

"THE FIRST SEAL"

Concerning the first seal, John said, "I watched as the Lamb opened the first of the seven seals. Then I heard one of the four living creatures say in a voice like thunder, 'Come!' I looked, and there before me was a white horse! Its rider held a bow, and he was given a crown, and he rode out as a conqueror bent on conquest"(Rev 6:1–2). This horseman is not to be confused by the rider of the white horse in Rev 19:11–16. This white horse is ridden by Jesus, being called Faithful and True, who judges and wages war with justice.

The first horseman is, in fact, evil. Many refer to him as the antichrist. Daniel showed the evil counterfeit in this way. Daniel 7:13–14 tells us, "I saw in the night visions, and, behold, one like the Son of man came with the clouds of heaven, and came to the Ancient of days, and they brought him near before him. And there was given him dominion, and glory, and a kingdom, that all people, nations, and languages, should serve him." He will conquer the world and require all to worship him. Only God will defeat him.

"THE SECOND SEAL"

The second seal had the power to kill. "When the Lamb opened the second seal, I heard the second living creature say, 'Come!' Then another horse came out, a fiery red one. Its rider was given power to take peace from the earth and to make people kill" (Rev 6:3–4). This sounds very much like the world at war: kingdom against kingdom. For the people of earth, this was nothing new. In Genesis, the first murder happened. Cain killed Abel because of sin and jealousy. Genesis 4:9–10 described this. "Then the Lord said to Cain, 'Where is your brother Abel?' 'I don't know,' he replied. 'Am I my brother's keeper?' The Lord said, 'What have you done? Listen! Your brother's blood cries out to me from the ground.'" Murder was also described in Jas 4:2. This disciple wrote, "You desire but do not have, so you kill. You covet but you cannot get what you want, so you quarrel and fight. You do not have because you do not ask God."

Moses, the author of the book of Leviticus, in the Old Testament, conveyed that God will allow war and death because his people refuse to listen to him. Moses understood that God would be a just God, but he also described what will happen to mankind because they will continue to disobey. "And I will bring a sword against you that will execute the vengeance of the covenant; when you are gathered together within your cities I will send pestilence among you; and you shall be delivered into the hand of the enemy"(Lev 26:25). Jesus is prepared to allow for wars and rumors of war to continue until his return. Again, it was Matt 24:6–7 that warned, "And ye shall hear of wars and rumors of wars: see that ye be not troubled: for all these things must come to pass, but the end is not yet. For nation shall rise against nation, and kingdom against kingdom: and there shall be famines, and pestilences, and earthquakes, in divers places." Jesus will open the second seal for the sake of justice and redemption.

"THE THIRD SEAL"

"When the Lamb opened the third seal, I heard the third living creature say, 'Come!' I looked, and there before me was a black horse! Its rider was holding a pair of scales in his hand" (Rev 6:5). Like Zechariah's prophecy of the different riders on horses of different colors, John also saw a black horse, which symbolized the judgment and famine that would come to the world. In Rev 6, the black horse is the third horseman of the apocalypse. Because it is also logical that war in our world would bring about famine, then it is also believable that the black horse rider represented famine. John told us, "And when he had opened the third seal, I heard the third beast say, Come and see. And I beheld, and lo a black horse; and he that sat on him had a pair of balances in his hand. And I heard a voice in the midst of the four beasts say, A measure of wheat for a denarius [penny], and three measures of barley for a penny; and see thou hurt not the oil and the wine" (Rev 6:5–6).

These verses seem to argue that wars and rumors of wars have the negative outcome of inflation because demands are never met by the supply needed. The people affected by this war would soon run out of food and money. Soon there would be widespread famine. This famine would obviously concern itself with foods and basic needs, but it would also be a time of spiritual famine. In Amos 8:11, the Old Testament prophet signals this. "The time is surely coming," says the Sovereign Lord, "when I will send a famine on the land—not a famine of bread or water but of hearing the words of the Lord." This prophecy was seen in the Old Testament but definitely is appropriate for the end of days.

As far as the verse talking about the penny and measure of barley, we must look at life in the first century. During that time, a denarius was equal to the daily wage made by one person. The "measure of barley" would not be enough to supply a man's hunger. This voice, which was heard from heaven, also declared that oil and wine not be touched. Even in a time when the antichrist brings war and famine, God is merciful. He puts limits on what the devil, the first horseman, and his riders, War and Famine, can do to mankind even in the last days.

"THE FOURTH SEAL"

The fourth horse of the apocalypses was a pale horse. Revelation 6:7–8 explains the fourth seal: "When the Lamb opened the fourth seal, I heard the voice of the fourth living creature say, 'Come!' I looked, and there before me was a pale horse! Its rider was named Death, and Hades was following close behind him. They were given power over a fourth of the earth to kill by sword, famine and plague, and by the wild beasts of the earth." In Dan 9:13–15 the prophet is describing the plagues and the reason for them. This was the meaning of why the Jews suffered while being held captive in Egypt. The verses, however, point to a coming time where disobedience to God causes the same effect.

> All this plague is come upon us, as it is written in the Law of Moses: yet made we not our prayer before the Lord our God, that we might turn from our iniquities and understand thy truth. Therefore hath the Lord made ready the plague, and brought it upon us: for the Lord our God is righteous in all his works which he does: for we would not hear his voice. And now, O Lord our God, that hast brought thy people out of the land of Egypt with a mighty hand, and hast gotten thee renown, as appeareth this day, we have sinned, we have done wickedly.

In these last days mankind has not learned to obey God. They have heard and known what God has done for people but will not listen to his word.

There would be much confusion during the last days. These horsemen usher in the battle between God and Satan. The book of Ezekiel in the Old Testament lists the four horsemen as sword, famine, wild beasts, and pestilence or plague, and they all cause confusion on the earth. Ezekiel 38:21 foretells this confusion. "I will call for a sword against Gog throughout all My mountains, says the Lord God. Every man's sword will be against his brother." Zechariah 12:4 states, "'In that day,' says the Lord, 'I will strike every horse with confusion, and its rider with madness; I will open My eyes on the house of Judah, and will strike every horse of the peoples with blindness.'" In Zech 14:13 the prophet wrote, "It shall come to pass in that day that a great panic from the Lord will be among them. Everyone will seize the hand of his neighbor, and raise his hand against his neighbor's hand."

The death rate will be astronomical. One-fourth of the world will die because of war and famine and by the beasts of the earth. These beasts may literally be dangerous animals but could also describe the kingdoms that have turned on the people of Israel and the people believing in Jesus.

Daniel, in chapters 7 and 8, describes four beasts from the sea and the one from the land. Daniel foretold what we read in John's vision. "And the ten horns which thou sawest are ten kings, which have received no kingdom as yet; but receive power as kings one hour with the beast. These have one mind, and shall give their power and strength unto the beast" (Rev 17:12–13). Daniel also saw the beast from the land who followed the other. "He had two horns like a lamb, but he spoke like a dragon. He exercised all the authority of the first beast on his behalf, and made the earth and its inhabitants worship the first beast, whose fatal wound had been healed" (Rev 13:11–12). Daniel's visions from God gave us a look at who would join with the antichrist to eliminate Christians and Jews.

"THE FIFTH SEAL"

In Rev 6:9–11 the fifth seal is opened. "When he opened the fifth seal, I saw under the altar the souls of those who had been slain because of the word of God and the testimony they had maintained. They called out in a loud voice, 'How long, Sovereign Lord, holy and true, until you judge the inhabitants of the earth and avenge our blood.' Then each of them was given a white robe, and they were told to wait a little longer, until the full number of their fellow servants, their brothers and sisters, were killed just as they had been." These martyred Christians are the ones who keep their belief in the Lord while being hunted by the antichrist and his minions during the tribulation.

The deceiver, spoken of time and again by John, is the antichrist. The disciple John writes that anyone can be an antichrist. He said, "Who is the liar? It is whoever denies that Jesus is the Christ. Such a person is the Antichrist denying the Father and the Son" (1 John 2:22). Satan will control the unbelievers on earth and these evil people will do his biding. In John 16:2–3 the author states that "the time is coming when anyone who kills you will think they are offering a service to God. They will do such things because they have not known the Father."

Daniel 7:25 also describes the antichrist. The prophet records the words God has given him. "He will speak against the Most High and oppress his holy people and try to change the set times and the laws. The holy people will be delivered into his hands for a time, times and half a time," meaning seven years. His prophecy continues as he explains the antichrist's peace treaty, which he will break halfway through the seven-year tribulation. "He will make a firm covenant with many for one week, but in the middle of the week he will put a stop to sacrifice and offering" (Dan 9:27).

"THE SIXTH SEAL"

John recorded his next vision. "I looked when He opened the sixth seal, and behold, there was a great earthquake; and the sun became black as sackcloth of hair, and the moon became like blood. And the stars of heaven fell to the earth, as a fig tree drops its late figs when it is shaken by a mighty wind" (Rev 6:12, 13). What he saw describes planetary and celestial destruction, the likes of which have never been seen before on earth. John saw earthquakes grander than they have ever been in history. He saw the sun disappear, and the moon turned to the color of blood red. Imagine if the vision that John saw were to come true, literally. Earthquakes would be felt throughout the entire world. There would be a total eclipse of the sun at the same time the moon would become blood red. If natural disasters like this happened, then the earth would produce such a dust cloud of dirt and debris the outcome would be exactly as John observed in his vision.

Not surprisingly, the prophets of old foretold of these disasters. Isaiah prophesied this in chapter 24:18–20, writing:

> And it shall come to pass, that he who fleeth from the noise of the fear shall fall into the pit; and he that cometh up out of the midst of the pit shall be taken in the snare: for the windows from on high are open, and the foundations of the earth do shake. The earth is utterly broken down, the earth is clean dissolved, the earth is moved exceedingly. The earth shall reel to and fro like a drunkard, and shall be removed like a cottage; and the transgression thereof shall be heavy upon it; and it shall fall, and not rise again.

The prophet Joel, in Joel 2:10, said, "The earth quakes before them; the heavens tremble; the sun and the moon are darkened; and the stars withdraw their shining." In Joel 2:31 he wrote, "The sun will be turned to darkness and the moon to blood before the coming of the great and dreadful day of the Lord." Isaiah 13:10 said, "For the stars of heaven and the constellations thereof shall not give their light: the sun shall be darkened in his going forth, and the moon shall not cause her light to shine." All of this was happening for one reason. Jesus was about to come back to earth and defeat Satan, get rid of evil, set up his kingdom on earth, and bring about the millennium.

"THE SEVENTH SEAL"

The seventh seal was opened and John hears—silence! Nothing! Not a word! Not a sound! Jesus is about to come back, but not as a baby wrapped in swaddling clothes and lying in a manger. He is not the Jesus who simply taught peace and love. He is not the gentle healer and perfect Lamb being led to slaughter on the cross. He is not here to convince people to repent and give their lives to him. Everything has changed. Jesus is coming as a conquering King, and he is returning with all of his angels. He is taking his place as the King of kings and revealing his glory and the glory of his angels. In Matt 25:31 it states that "when the Son of Man comes in his glory, and all the angels with him, he will sit on his glorious throne." The prophecies of the seven seals had finally been fulfilled, and Jesus was ready to set up his heavenly kingdom on earth. John showed us his vision by explaining:

> When he opened the seventh seal, there was silence in heaven for about half an hour. And I saw the seven angels who stand before God, and seven trumpets were given to them. Another angel, who had a golden censer, came and stood at the altar. He was given much incense to offer, with the prayers of all God's people, on the golden altar in front of the throne. The smoke of the incense, together with the prayers of God's people, went up before God from the angel's hand. Then the angel took the censer, filled it with fire from the altar, and hurled it on the earth; and there came peals of thunder, rumblings, flashes of lightning and an earthquake. Then the seven angels who had the seven trumpets prepared to sound them.

This seventh seal signaled the seven angels holding the seven trumpets, who then signaled the seven angels to pour out their bowls of judgment on the earth.

Chapter 15

SEVEN BOWLS OF JUDGMENT

THE SEVEN BOWLS OF JUDGMENTS are the final judgments at the end of the tribulation. Nothing on earth has ever seen God's wrath in the way it is about to be displayed. When these bowls have finally been emptied out, the earth will be all but destroyed. This will begin as the antichrist breaks his seven-year treaty with Israel. Satan will gather many nations to go against the people of Israel who had believed he had brought peace to them. He, actually, has planned the death of all of Israel and all who follow Yahweh or Jesus. Ezekiel foretold of this disaster in Ezek 38:1–6:

> The word of the Lord came to me: "Son of man, set your face against Gog, of the land of Magog, the chief prince of Meshek and Tubal; prophesy against him and say: 'This is what the Sovereign Lord says: I am against you, Gog, chief prince of Meshek and Tubal. I will turn you around, put hooks in your jaws and bring you out with your whole army—your horses, your horsemen fully armed, and a great horde with large and small shields, all of them brandishing their swords. Persia, Cush and Put will be with them, all with shields and helmets, also Gomer with all its troops, and Beth Togarmah from the far north with all its troops—the many nations with you."

The antichrist will gather together many nations from around the world to surround Israel with plans to wipe them off the face of the earth. Christians coming to Jesus after the rapture will also be targeted. Ezekiel prophesied that this would happen in the far future. He explained which nations would attack and who they would be attacking. "In future years you will invade a land that has recovered from war, whose people were gathered from many nations to the mountains of Israel, which had long been desolate. They had been brought out from the nations, and now all of them live in safety [Satan's promise for a seven-year peace]. You and all your troops and the many nations with you will go up, advancing like a storm; you will be like a cloud covering the land" (Ezek 38:8–9). Satan will have raised a world-wide army for his purpose. He will break the peace treaty half way through the seven years. It is then that the seven bowls of wrath will be poured out. John described the first bowl. It was a plague that is to be poured out, "and ugly, festering sores broke out on the people who had the mark of the beast and worshiped its image" (Rev 16:2). These plagues come against all the people who have decided to follow and worship the antichrist Those people who, during the tribulation, have accepted Jesus will not be affected by this plague. Again it is Daniel, in a way, who foretold this. Daniel 9:13–14 says, "All this plague is come upon us, as it is written in the Law of Moses: yet made we not our prayer before the Lord our God, that we might turn from our iniquities and understand thy truth. Therefore hath the Lord made ready the plague, and brought it upon us: for the Lord our God is righteous in all his works which he doeth: for we would not hear his voice."

Those, like the followers of the antichrist, who do not listen to God have experienced this plague before. In the time of Moses, the pharaoh of Egypt refused to free the people of Israel. Exodus 9:8–12 shows the once and future wrath of God. "Then the Lord said to Moses and Aaron, 'Take handfuls of soot from a furnace and have Moses toss it into the air in the presence of Pharaoh. It will become fine dust over the whole land of Egypt, and festering boils will break out on people and animals throughout the land.'"

The second act of wrath will be poured out onto the sea. The water will turn "into blood like that of a dead person, and every living thing in the sea died" (Rev 16:3). One-third of the living creatures in the sea had already perished when the second trumpet sounded. Now, there was no life at all in the oceans. The waters turning to blood also reminds us of the Old Testament story of Moses. Once again, pharaoh refused to listen to God. He showed his power by turning water into blood. Moses told pharaoh, in Exod 7:17, "So this is what the Lord says: 'I will show you that I am the Lord.' Look! I will strike the water of the Nile with this staff in my hand, and the river will turn to blood. The fish in it will die." Although not a direct prophecy, the stories are quite similar.

The third bowl mirrors the second. When the third bowl of God's wrath is poured out, the rivers and springs also turn to blood. "And I heard an angel of the waters say, Lord, thou art just, which art, and which was, and holy because thou hast judged these things" (Rev 16:5). Verses 6 and 7 continue with the angel of the water and the answer given by another angel. "'For they have shed the blood of saints and prophets, and You have given them blood to drink. For it is their just due.' And I heard another from the altar saying, 'Even so, Lord God Almighty, true and righteous are Your judgments.'"

John then observes the fourth angel pouring out his bowl on the sun. Revelation 16:8–9 said, "Then the fourth angel poured out his bowl on the sun, and power was given to him to scorch men with fire. And men were scorched with great heat, and they blasphemed the name of God who has power over these plagues; and they did not repent and give Him glory." The evilness of the people was not unexpected. It began when people turned and decided to be lovers of themselves.

Saint Timothy had explained the importance of preaching the gospel and what would happen to those who refused the words and refused to listen.

> Now the Spirit expressly says that in later times some will renounce the faith by paying attention to deceitful spirits and teachings of demons, through the hypocrisy of liars whose consciences are seared with a hot iron. They forbid marriage and demand abstinence from foods, which God created to be received with thanksgiving by those who believe and know the truth. For everything created by God is good, and nothing is to be rejected, provided it is received with thanksgiving: for it is sanctified by God's word and by prayer. (1 Tim 4:1–5)

These verses are actually prophecies of what has happened in our own time. People no longer want to hear or believe God's word.

The fifth bowl of wrath causes the earth, which is controlled by Satan, to be covered by a great darkness. The pain and suffering of the wicked are multiplied as each bowl is poured onto the kingdom of the beast (Satan). "The people gnawed their tongues in agony, and cursed the God of heaven because of their pains and sores, and they did not repent of their deeds" (Rev 16:11). These followers of the antichrist, filled with evil, refused to repent and believe.

The life of Moses is once again like looking into a mirror. In Egypt, because of refusal to listen to the word of God, the Lord took away the light. Exodus 10:21–23 shows this fifth bowl. "Then the Lord said to Moses, 'Stretch out your hand towards heaven so that there may be darkness over the land of Egypt, a darkness that can be felt.' So Moses stretched out his hand towards heaven, and there was dense darkness in all the land of Egypt for three days. People could not see one another, and for three days they could not move from where they were." We all remember the story of Moses and how pharaoh eventually listened to Moses and let God's people go. The plagues ended with the freedom of the Jews.

At the time of the end, the followers of the antichrist will not listen. In the first place, it is their fault that these bowls of wrath have been poured out. One would think that they would call out to God and ask for mercy. All they need do is repent, but they will not! Proverbs 19:13 sums it up best. "One's own folly leads to ruin, yet the heart rages against the Lord." It is the deeds of the wicked, in the end times, that have brought them to ruin. Rather than pleading for mercy, they curse God. Proverbs 19:9 easily explains, "The fear of the LORD is pure, enduring forever; the judgments of the LORD are true, being altogether righteous."

Now, the sixth bowl poured out its judgment on the Euphrates river. The river dried up, causing a way for the armies of the devil to begin their attack on Israel. The Bible describes it in Rev 16:12. "Then the sixth angel poured out his bowl on the great river Euphrates, and its water was dried up, so that the way of the kings from the east might be prepared." The Battle of Armageddon was about to begin.

After John saw the sixth bowl, he observed three filthy spirits. To him they looked like frogs coming from the mouths of Satan, the dragon, and the false prophet. He describes this vision in Rev 16:13–16.

> And I saw three unclean spirits like frogs coming out of the mouth of the dragon, out of the mouth of the beast, and out of the mouth of the false prophet. For they are spirits of demons, performing signs, which go out to the kings of the earth and of the whole world, to gather them to the battle of that great day of God Almighty. "Behold, I am coming as a thief. Blessed is he who watches, and keeps his garments, lest he walk naked and they see his shame." And they gathered them together to the place called in Hebrew, Armageddon.

Isaiah, long ago, prophesied this upcoming battle. In Isa 13:4–6 he prophesied this: "The noise of a multitude in the mountains, like that of many people! A tumultuous noise of the kingdoms of nations gathered together! The Lord of hosts musters the army for battle. They come from a far country, from the end of heaven—The Lord and His weapons of indignation, to destroy the whole land. Wail, for the day of the Lord is at hand! It will come as destruction from the Almighty."

Jesus, then, will be gathering together all the forces of heaven, including the angels and those who had been faithful and were taken up during the rapture. His army is ready to fight the beast's army, the vast army of the kings of the east, and all the other nations from around the world. This will be the final battle between man and God.

> Then the seventh angel poured out his bowl into the air, and a loud voice came out of the temple of heaven, from the throne, saying, "It is done!" And there were noises and thundering and lightnings; and there was a great earthquake, such a mighty and great earthquake as had not occurred since men were on the earth. Now the great city was divided into three parts, and the cities of the nations fell. And great Babylon was remembered before God, to give her the cup of the wine of the fierceness of His wrath. Then every island fled away, and the mountains were not found. And great hail from heaven fell upon men, each hailstone about the weight of a talent. Men blasphemed God because of the plague of the hail, since that plague was exceedingly great. (Rev 16:17–21)

Ezekiel had predicted this exact event in Ezek 36:22–23 and explained the reason behind the battle. "I will execute judgment on him with plague and bloodshed; I will pour down torrents of rain, hailstones and burning sulfur on him and on his troops and on the many nations with him. Thus I will magnify Myself and sanctify Myself, and I will be known in the eyes of many nations. Then they shall know that I am the Lord."

The prophet Amos also saw the end. "The Lord God of hosts, He who touches the earth and it melts, and all who dwell there mourn." All of the prophets told of the steps God had to take to defeat Satan and the wicked who had taken over the earth. If he had not, there would be nothing left of the world. Matthew, in chapter 24, verse 21, explains. "And unless those days were shortened, no flesh would be saved; but for the elect's sake those days will be shortened."

The wrath of God had been poured out, in John's vision. Jesus was now to take his place as King of kings. The first time Jesus came to earth, he came as a servant. He was a baby, born for one reason and one reason only. He was taking man's sins upon himself on a cross. He was prepared to die to defeat death. Because he was the sacrificial Lamb, he came to provide the way to heaven to all who believed. This was the first advent. In the second advent, Jesus comes as the sovereign Lord of lords, King of kings, and the God above all gods. He is going to set up his kingdom in Jerusalem after the complete defeat of Satan. When he does come down, to defeat the forces of evil, the entire world will see him appear. Matthew 24:30 shows how. "Then the sign of the Son of Man will appear in heaven, and then all the tribes of the earth will mourn, and they will see the Son of Man coming on the clouds of heaven with power and great glory." This coming in power and glory will bring in the millennium. Ezekiel prophesied what Jesus would say. "I will set My glory among the nations; all the nations shall see My judgment which I have executed, and My hand which I have laid on them" (Ezek 39:21).

CHAPTER 16

A NEW HEAVEN AND
A NEW EARTH

JESUS WILL BE VICTORIOUS and will defeat the wicked who follow the anti-christ, and he will punish Satan. He will set up his kingdom for a thousand years. What will happen is found in the vision John had about the victory of the Lord. It is best described in Rev 20, where John explained that the millennium (one thousand years) begins after the second coming of Jesus. It is a time when the Christ will reign, bringing peace and righteousness. The people who had survived the tribulation, without losing faith, will be filled with joy because it will be the first time they actually see the Savior. John recorded his vision.

> And I saw an angel coming down out of heaven, having the key to the Abyss and holding in his hand a great chain. He seized the dragon, that ancient serpent, who is the devil, or Satan, and bound him for a thousand years. He threw him into the Abyss, and locked and sealed it over him, to keep him from deceiving the nations anymore until the thousand years were ended. After that, he must be set free for a short time. I saw thrones on which were seated those who had been given authority to judge. And I saw the souls of those who had been beheaded because of their testimony about Jesus and because of the word of God. They had not worshiped the beast or its image and had not received its mark on their fore-heads or their hands. They came to life and reigned with Christ a thousand years. (The rest of the dead did not come to life until the thousand years were ended.) This is the first resurrection. Blessed

and holy are those who share in the first resurrection. The second death has no power over them, but they will be priests of God and of Christ and will reign with him for a thousand years. (Rev 20:1–6)

First, John saw an angel coming down with the keys to the abyss. The book of Isa 24:21 talked about this occasion thousands of years before it is supposed to happen. "In that day the Lord will punish the powers in the heavens above and the kings on the earth below. They will be herded together like prisoners bound in a dungeon; they will be shut up in prison and be punished after many days . . . for the Lord Almighty will reign on Mount Zion and in Jerusalem, and before its elders—with great glory."

The prison John referred to is also found in Isaiah and is called the bottomless pit. The Greek translation is "abyss" and means that it is unbounded, a depth that cannot be measured, a pit without a bottom. Imagine the universe before creation. Genesis 1:2 tells us that "in the beginning, God created the Heavens and the earth. The earth was without form, and void." The universe, before creation, was an abyss. This abyss will be the holding place of Satan (the beast), the dragon (the false prophet), demons, and those with the mark. Next, John sees the thrones given to those with the authority to judge. The followers who have been faithful to the end will be rewarded. Revelation 3:21 has John describing the promise of Jesus. "He who overcomes, I will grant to him to sit down with Me on My throne, as I also overcame and sat down with my Father in His throne." Those chosen will more than likely be the ones who were martyred because they walked with Jesus in the face of death. Revelation 20:4 may be describing them. "And I saw the souls of them that had been beheaded for the witness of Jesus and for the Word of God, and who had not worshiped the beast, nor his image, nor had received his mark upon their foreheads or on their hands; and they lived and reigned with Christ a thousand years."

There are, according to the Revelation of John, those who only experience the first death. Their bodies have died, but their spirit and soul will never see death because they belong to the Messiah. Those who did not accept Jesus will suffer the second death after the pit. The second death will be far worse. It is a spiritual death in which the followers of Satan will find themselves separated from God.

They will be tormented forever, and this death is irreversible. It is those who will never suffer the second death who will reign and live with God for a thousand years.

The end, however, is not yet. What will happen during those thousand years when the Messiah is on his throne? What will happen to those who were dead in Christ and those who were true believers, taken up during the rapture? To begin with, there will be humans who survived during the seven years of tribulation who did not accept the mark of the beast or worship him. Those people will be told by some of the believers who came back with Jesus about the Lord and what he had done for them. Salvation work will continue. Not everyone is lost beyond all hope.

We will never know the full details of the one-thousand-year reign, but those who took the mark of the beast (the lawless one) will be lost. In 2 Thess 2:3–4, Paul reminds us not to be deceived by Satan. "Don't let anyone deceive you in any way, for that day will not come until the rebellion occurs and the man of lawlessness is revealed, the man doomed to destruction. He will oppose and will exalt himself over everything that is called God or is worshiped, so that he sets himself up in God's temple, proclaiming himself to be God." We have been told from the beginning, we have been warned by followers of Christ, and we will have had the opportunity to see the truth before the war between God and Satan. Everyone left, after the rapture, will have had the chance to choose. The vision of John has been shared and "this calls for endurance and faithfulness on the part of God's people" (Rev 14:12). During the takeover of the world by Satan, there will be witnesses who explain the supernatural acts of the beast. There will be 144,000 Jews, 12,000 from each of the 12 tribes, who have turned to the Messiah, Jesus, and will have proclaimed the truth of God's word. Even an angel in heaven will have preached the gospel. "And I saw another angel fly in the midst of heaven, having the everlasting gospel to preach unto them that dwell on the earth, and to every nation" (Rev 14:6). All mankind had the chance to choose which side to follow.

The millennium will be ruled over by Jesus. He will be the King of Israel and all the nations. Isaiah foretold of this time, too. In Isa 2:4, he wrote, "He will judge between the nations and will settle disputes for many peoples. They will beat their swords into plowshares and their spears into pruning hooks. Nation will not take up sword against nation, nor will they train for war anymore."

God will fulfill all the covenants that he ever made to the people of the earth, during this time. He will keep his promises made to Israel, to Jesus, to the nations, and to creation. The land promised to the Jews will be realized. In Gen 15:18–20, the covenant was given. On that day the Lord made a covenant with Abram and said, "To your descendants I give this land, from the Wadi of Egypt to the great river, the Euphrates—the land of the Kenites, Kenizzites, Kadmonites, Hittites, Perizzites, Rephaites, Amorites, Canaanites, Girgashites and Jebusites."

Another covenant to be fulfilled was made with David. In 2 Sam 7:16, God said, "Your house and your kingdom will endure forever before me; your throne will be established forever." David will also have a throne. He will be a very important leader in the reign of the Christ. Jeremiah 31:33 tells us, "But this is the covenant that I will make with the house of Israel after those days, declares the LORD: I will put my law within them, and I will write it on their hearts. And I will be their God, and they shall be my people." Ezekiel 36:28 is more precise. "You shall dwell in the land that I gave to your fathers, and you shall be my people, and I will be your God." Israel will reconcile with God and God with Israel. Not every Jew will be saved, but Israel, as a nation, will all worship Jesus, the Messiah. They will be in the thousand-year reign of Christ.

God made other covenants to the people of earth. Creation, itself, was given a promise. In Rom 8:18–23, Paul explained. "I consider that our present sufferings are not worth comparing with the glory that will be revealed in us. For the creation waits in eager expectation for the children of God to be revealed. For the creation was subjected to frustration, not by its own choice, but by the will of the one who subjected it, in hope that the creation itself will be liberated from its bondage to decay and brought into the freedom and glory of the children of God." The curse of creation will be lifted.

The earth as well as all of the animals will be restored. Peace will reign. Isaiah 11:6–9 tells what will happen during the thousand-year reign.

> The wolf will live with the lamb, the leopard will lie down with the goat, the calf and the lion and the yearling together; and a little child will lead them. The cow will feed with the bear, their young will lie down together, and the lion will eat straw like the ox. The infant will play near the cobra's den, and the young child will put its hand into the viper's nest. They will neither harm nor destroy on all my holy mountain, for the earth will be filled with the knowledge of the Lord as the waters cover the sea.

I believe that during Christ's kingdom, there will be no more disease or death. Peace will abound and life will continue. We will work, eat, sleep, and live in peace and the love of our God.

The thousand-year reign of Jesus will be without the devil in our presence. This, though, is not the end of Satan's attempt to be victorious over God. John told us what would happen after the millennium: "after that he must be let loose for a little while" (Rev 20:2–3). Whether he is released to give him one more chance or whether God is showing mankind that there is no hope for Satan, he will once again try to take souls. This time, will be his last. At the end of the millennium:

> When the thousand years are ended, Satan will be let loose from his prison, and he will come out to seduce the nations in the four quarters of the earth. He will muster them for war, the hosts of Gog and Magog, countless as the sands of the sea. They marched up over the breadth of the land and laid siege to the camp of God's people and the city He loves. But fire came down on them from heaven and consumed them. Their seducer, the Devil, was flung into the lake of fire and sulfur where the beast and the false prophet are. (Rev 20:7–10)

God's punishment, this time, will be permanent.

It is then that the great judgment will occur. John explained it this way. Revelation 20:11–15 told us all what John saw.

> And I saw a great white throne, and him that sat upon it, from whose face the earth and the heaven fled away; and there was found no place for them. And I saw the dead, the great and the small, standing before the throne; and books were opened: and another book was opened, which is the book of life: and the dead were judged out of the things which were written in the books, according to their works. And the sea gave up the dead that were in it; and death and Hades gave up the dead that were in them: and they were judged every man according to their works. And death and Hades were cast into the lake of fire. This is the second death, even the lake of fire. And if any was not found written in the book of life, he was cast into the lake of fire.

The fact that one's name is found in the Book of Life is dependent on the life that someone has led. This will encompass billions and billions of people from the time of Adam to the generation that was alive during the millennium. All will be judged, but some may be acquitted. The decision of punishment will end in separation of the wicked and the righteous. Indeed, many will face punishment, but many more will have their names entered into the Book of Life.

The decision seems to be based on two criteria. Revelation 20:12 has explained that "the dead were judged out of the things which were written in the books" and "according to their works." The term here for "the books" seems to refer to the Holy Scripture. These people will be judged by the Bible's criterion for righteousness. The second criterion is based on works. By looking at both criteria, those who did the work of God before the birth of Jesus would have the same chance as those who had been born after. Many followed the words in the Old Testament and never had the opportunity to find the salvation given in the Gospels. Those who lived before Jesus will get the opportunity to find the Messiah. Matthew was discussing this when Jesus had performed miracles . . . in cities such as Chorazin, Bethsaida, and Capernaum. He rebuked those people because they would not believe and repent. Jesus said, "And you, Capernaum, . . . if the mighty works which were done in you had been done in Sodom, it would have remained until this day . . . . It shall be more tolerable for the land of Sodom in the day of judgment than for you" (Matt 11:23–24).

After the final judgment, there will be a new heaven and a new earth (Rev 21:1). This is where paradise will be known and understood. Those who have been found in the Book of Life will enter eternity and be able to communicate with God directly, just as Adam did while living in Eden. John reveals for us, in chapters 21 and 22, the new heaven and earth and who will inherit this paradise. John tells us what God said. "He who overcomes shall inherit all things, and I will be his God and he shall be My son" (Rev 21:7). Paul wrote in Rom 8:17, "and if children, then heirs; heirs of God, and joint-heirs with Christ; if so be that we suffer with him, that we may be also glorified with him."

What will we be like? According to John, we will become like Jesus Christ. First John 3:1–2 explained. "See what great love the Father has lavished on us, that we should be called children of God! And that is what we are! The reason the world does not know us is that it did not know him. Dear friends, now we are children of God, and what we will be has not yet been made known. But we know that when Christ appears, we shall be like him, for we shall see him as he is." Even Paul, who suffered and died for following and teaching the words of the Messiah, said, "The sufferings of this present time are not worthy to be compared with the glory which shall be revealed in us when we inherit all things" (Rom 8:18).

It is during this time, that these new heirs will populate this new heaven and earth. These are the children of God, who Paul described, and "who are miraculously changed into immortal spirit beings."[1] First Corinthians 15:51–54 is explicit. "When the perishable has been clothed with the imperishable, and the mortal with immortality, then the saying that is written will come true: Death has been swallowed up in victory." Paul is mirroring Isaiah here because the prophet had written "he will swallow up death in victory; and the Lord GOD will wipe away tears from off all faces; and the rebuke of his people shall he take away from off all the earth: for the LORD hath spoken it" (Isa 25:8). It is then that God will be with mankind and mankind with God.

John saw a new Jerusalem descend from heaven. This new city will hold what Gal 6:16 called the "true Israel of God." Isaiah prophesies frequently concern the future—not his future, but the world's future. He even explained the new Jerusalem. Although some people tell us that Isaiah is merely talking about going to the house of the Lord in his time, it is his first line that explains he is prophesying about the future. Isaiah 2:1–5 says, "It shall come to pass in the latter days that the mountain of the house of the Lord shall be established as the highest of the mountains, and shall be raised above the hills; and all the nations shall flow to it, and many peoples shall come, and say: 'Come, let us go up to the mountain of the Lord, to the house of the God of Jacob; that he may teach us his ways and that we may walk in his paths. For out of Zion shall go forth the law, and the word of the Lord from Jerusalem.'"

Ezekiel, too, foretold the coming of the New Jerusalem In chapter 48:35, God's new Jerusalem will be the place where the heirs of Jesus will come from all the world's nations, and this place will serve as the capital of the kingdom of Israel where the great throne will be found. Ezekiel told us in verse 35 that "the name of the city from that day shall be, 'The Lord is there.'" The prophet almost painted a picture of the "temple" from where Jesus will rule. He explained the outer courtyards and how they led into the inner courtyard. He told of a three-story building that is the temple, and an altar sat in front of that. The steps then led to the door that opened to the holy place and then to the most holy place. The temple rooms were made of wood. On the walls were palm trees and cherub angels carved into the wood. There were many rooms and buildings where the priests would abide, south and north of the temple. Ezekiel saw a temple building and described it as best he could, seeing only a vision of far off, future things.

Revelation 21:17–21 completes this picture.

1. United Church of God, "Beyond the Millennium."

And he [the angel] measured its wall, 144 cubits, by human measurements, which are also angelic measurements. The material of the wall was jasper; and the city was pure gold, like clear glass. The foundation stones of the city wall were decorated with every kind of precious stone. The first foundation stone was jasper; the second, sapphire; the third, chalcedony; the fourth, emerald; the fifth, sardonyx; the sixth, sardius; the seventh, chrysolite; the eighth, beryl; the ninth, topaz; the tenth, chrysoprase; the eleventh, jacinth; the twelfth, amethyst. And the twelve gates were twelve pearls; each one of the gates was a single pearl. And the street of the city was pure gold, like transparent glass.

The new Jerusalem, according to John's vision shows

. . . no temple in it, for the Lord God the Almighty and the Lamb are its temple. And the city has no need of the sun or of the moon to shine on it, for the glory of God has illuminated it, and its lamp is the Lamb. The nations will walk by its light, and the kings of the earth will bring their glory into it. In the daytime (for there will be no night there) its gates will never be closed; and they will bring the glory and the honor of the nations into it; and nothing unclean, and no one who practices abomination and lying, shall ever come into it, but only those whose names are written in the Lamb's book of life. (Rev 21:22–27)

The new Jerusalem will be a place of peace. People will live in harmony and there will be no more sin. It will be much like the garden of Eden flowing with life-giving rivers surrounding the tree of life. This city, in many ways, symbolizes the ultimate goal of every true believer in Jesus, the Messiah. Ever since Adam and Eve committed the first sin, mankind has been trying to find their way back to God. Genesis records them leaving the place where humans could actually be with God. The new Jerusalem shows the completed journey where mankind, who believe in the Messiah, return to be with the Lord. Revelation 22:6–7 begins the final message that John saw in his spirit-guided vision. "And he said to me, 'These words are faithful and true'; and the Lord, the God of the spirits of the prophets, sent His angel to show His bond-servants the things which must soon take place. 'And behold, I am coming quickly. Blessed is the one who keeps the words of the prophecy of this book.'" Jesus has shown that he is indeed the Savior of the world. Paul gave us this message in Rom 10:13: "For whoever calls on the name of the Lord shall be saved," and John, himself, stated, "For God so loved the world that he gave his one and only Son, that whoever believes in him shall not perish but have eternal life" (John 3:16). At the end of this vision, Christ is coming again. The Messiah will rule over his universe as he intended from the beginning. Mankind has been restored and is now a part of God's creation as it was meant to be.

Chapter 17

FINALE

REMEMBER THAT A PROPHECY that comes from God must come true. Isaiah spoke the words of God, and exempting the ones concerning events that have not happened, everything he claimed was the word of God came to pass. He was a prophet from God. It is easy, then, to think his prophecies that have yet to occur will actually happen. The other prophets of the Old Testament, too, in order to be considered presenting the word of God faithfully, needed to be just as correct as Isaiah. We have seen this fulfillment in Daniel, Ezekiel, Joel, Jeremiah, Elijah and Elisha, as well as the others. What they have recorded about the Messiah, from the beginning of time, his birth, his life, his death, and his resurrection—have all come true. Is it not easy to assume, then, that the prophecies that told about the rapture, his second coming, and the new Jerusalem are also true?

First, to believe that what these prophets said was actually a word from God, we must ask why they did what they did. These men of God were actually servants of Yahweh. What they said was what they were told to say. They knew what God had spoken and that it wasn't something from their own thoughts. Amos 3:7 conveyed this idea. "Surely the Sovereign Lord does nothing without revealing his plan to his servants the prophets."

God spoke to these prophets in different ways. Paul wrote, "God, who at various times and in different ways spoke in time past to the fathers by the prophets . . ." (Heb 1:1). Sometimes God spoke in dreams or in visions. "If there is a prophet among you, I, the Lord, make Myself known to him in a vision, and I speak to him in a dream" (Num 12:6). There were times when God spoke face to face to some of his servants. Moses, for example, was one who heard the word of God spoken. Elijah, too, knew it was the Lord that called him, because of a "still, small voice" (1 Kgs 19:12).

These men of Yahweh heard him speak and were intercessors between God and mankind. They were men who corrected people who had defiled and disobeyed the word of the Lord. Ezekiel, who was approached by God, explained:

> He [God] said to me, "Son of man, stand up on your feet and I will speak to you." As he spoke, the Spirit came into me and raised me to my feet, and I heard him speaking to me. He said: "Son of man, I am sending you to the Israelites, to a rebellious nation that has rebelled against me; they and their ancestors have been in revolt against me to this very day. The people to whom I am sending you are obstinate and stubborn. Say to them, 'This is what the Sovereign Lord says.' And whether they listen or fail to listen—for they are a rebellious people—they will know that a prophet has been among them." (Ezek 2:1–5)

Later, this prophet told God's people that the Lord had spoken. "I have sworn with uplifted hand that they must bear the consequences of their sin, declares the Sovereign Lord" (Ezek 44:12).

It was the prophets, too, who showed the power of God. Elijah believed in God's power and challenged Obadiah and Ahab, who had turned from God to worship Baal. Elijah told Ahab to gather the four hundred and fifty prophets of Baal. The challenge was to bring fire from heaven to burn a sacrifice. The prophet of God spoke to the people of Israel, "How long will you waver between two opinions? If the Lord is God, follow him; but if Baal is God, follow him" (1 Kgs 18:21). When everything was prepared, the worshipers of Baal asked their god to bring down fire. It didn't happen, not even a spark from heaven. When Elijah asked the God of Israel to bring down fire, the people saw the power of Yahweh.

> "Lord, the God of Abraham, Isaac and Israel, let it be known today that you are God in Israel and that I am your servant and have done all these things at your command. Answer me, Lord, answer me, so these people will know that you, Lord, are God, and that you are turning their hearts back again." Then the fire of the Lord fell and burned up the sacrifice, the wood, the stones and the soil, and also licked up water in the trench. When all the people saw this, they fell prostrate and cried, "The Lord—He is God! The Lord—he is God!" (1 Kgs 18:36–39)

Prophets did more than show the power of God to those who had sinned and turned away. They often foretold what would happen in the future. It has been described here how these prophets announced the coming of the Messiah. This has been shown by all the prophets, Moses, Daniel, Isaiah, Jeremiah, David, Micah, along with others who knew who Jesus would be, when he would come, and when he would return. These prophets were chosen because they were set apart from the rest of the world so that they could walk in obedience to the Lord. Jeremiah 1:5 said, "Before I formed you in the womb I knew you, before you were born I set you apart; I appointed you as a prophet to the nations."

The prophets of old were telling truth to a world looking for a way. It didn't matter whether it was about the people who needed to turn back to God, the good news concerning the Messiah's birth, or the second coming of Jesus to set up his kingdom. The prophets had a message and that message needed to come true. Jesus, in Luke 24:44, said to his disciples, "This is what I told you while I was still with you: Everything must be fulfilled that is written about me in the Law of Moses, the Prophets, and the Psalms." John has shown us the way to be a part of this new creation that is about to come upon the earth. In John 3:16, Jesus said, "For God so loved the world, that He gave His only Son, so that everyone who believes in Him will not perish, but have eternal life." From the beginning, in the book of Gen 1:26, the creator said, "Let us make humankind in our image, according to our likeness; let them have dominion over the fish of the sea, over the birds of the heavens, and over the livestock, and over all the earth, and over every creeping thing that creeps on the earth." This is where we realize that humans were created as independent beings with the ability to choose right from wrong, which is the definition of free will.

How then, do we become a part of the vision John was given to impart to us? Is there a place in your life for Jesus, the Messiah? Inside you know that the wages of sin is death. That started with Adam because he disobeyed God; he was told, in Gen 2:16–17, "Of every tree of the garden you may freely eat; but of the tree of the knowledge of good and evil you shall not eat, for in the day that you eat of it you shall surely die." Disobedience caused separation between man and God. Because we, too, have free will, we sin and the outcome is the same for us. Ezekiel told us, in his book, chapter 18:4, that "the soul who sins will die." James explained the reason we choose what we do. "Then when lust hath conceived, it bringeth forth sin; and sin, when it is finished, bringeth forth death" (Jas 1:15). It was Paul, however, who gave us the remedy in Rom 6:23: "For the wages of sin is death, but the gift of God is eternal life in Christ Jesus our Lord."

I will leave you with this: Jesus was with the disciples just before he ascended to heaven. He explained who he really was.

> "Let not your hearts be troubled. Believe in God; believe also in me. In my Father's house are many mansions. If it were not so, would I have told you that I go to prepare a place for you? And if I go and prepare a place for you, I will come again and will take you to myself, that where I am you may be also. And you know the way to where I am going." Thomas said to him, "Lord, we do not know where you are going. How can we know the way?" Jesus said to him, "I am the way, and the truth, and the life. No one comes to the Father except through me. If you had known me, you would have known my Father also. From now on you do know Him and have seen Him." (John 14:1–7)

You know that, just like me, you have done the opposite of what has been asked of us by God. Maybe, now, you wish to make things right with God. You, too, can join those who know the prophecies told about the Christ are the only way. I pray that you do. The prophets of old were correct. All we need do is ask Jesus. Simply talk to him and tell him you changed your mind about him. You could say, "Lord you are the Son of God and you are God. I am a sinner and I am sorry for the way I have been. You came into this world to show us the way we are to live and to provide eternal life to those who would repent of their sins and accept you. I do that now. Jesus, come into my life and live in my heart. I will give you all the glory. Thank you, God, for your promise. Amen!"

APPENDIX

The Apostles—Gave Their Lives for Jesus

MANY OF THE APOSTLES died for their faith in Jesus Christ. Some of these were eyewitnesses[1] who saw Jesus die and saw him as a risen Messiah. These followers of the Christ were willing to go to their deaths because they knew they would be with Jesus again. They died because they claimed to have seen Christ die and then saw him alive again. Their refusal to renounce their faith in Jesus is evidence that they truly witnessed the resurrection of Jesus Christ.

MEN MARTYRED FOR THEIR FAITH IN JESUS

MARTYR	DEATH
ANDREW	Martyred by crucifixion in Greece; said, "Cross, sanctified by the body of Christ Good Cross, long desired always, I loved you and wished to embrace you. Welcome me and bring me to my master."[2]
BARNABAS	Stoned by angry Jews or was bound with a rope by the neck and then dragged only to the site where he would be burned to death.
BAR-THOLOMEW	Martyred by being skinned alive and beheaded at the orders of Armenian King Astyages. This was due to his refusal to worship the local pagan gods.

1. The following facts are taken from McDowell, "Did the Apostles Really Die"; and Sharefaith Team, "20 Christian Women Who Died."

2. Saint of the Day, "St. Andrew the Apostle."

JAMES	First apostle killed in Jerusalem, by the sword; said to have spoken about the end of his life, including his death, prayer, and resurrection.
JAMES	Brother of Jesus; martyred in AD 62 or 69 by being stoned or clubbed to death on the order of High Priest Ananus ben Ananus.
JOHN	Boiled in oil but did not die; preached until his natural death; John is believed to have died a very old man in Ephesus (Turkey) around AD 100; he did not die for his faith—the only disciple not to die for his faith.
JUDAS	Committed suicide after the betrayal of Jesus. "I have sinned, for I have betrayed innocent blood" (Matt 27:4).
MATTHEW	Lived more than twenty years after the death of Christ; killed at the altar with a sword in the back in Parthia (Iran).
MATTHIAS	Was stoned and then beheaded.
NICANOR	Stoned the same day as Stephen.
PAUL	Beheaded in Rome in 66 AD by Nero.
PETER	Crucified upside down around AD 66 by Nero because he said he was not worthy to be crucified the same way as our Lord.
PHILIP THE APOSTLE	Martyred by a Roman proconsul angry because his wife converted to Christianity; continued preaching while upside down, and the crowd offered to free him, but he refused.
PHILIP THE DEACON	Confused with the Philip the apostle; actually one of the seven chosen in Acts 6:7; died in the first century AD.
SIMON THE ZEALOT	Half brother of Jesus; martyred by being cut in half with a saw.
STEPHEN	Stoned to death in Jerusalem.
THADDEUS (JUDE)	Beaten to death with a club, then beheaded, his body axed to pieces.
THOMAS	Stabbed in India by four soldiers. Thomas touched Jesus' side where the sword pierced him—Thomas suffered the same fate!
TIMON	Saint Timon died by crucifixion after being thrown in a red hot furnace and, protected by God, emerging unharmed. Later he was crucified.
TIMOTHY	Tried to halt a procession in honor of the goddess Diana by preaching the gospel. The angry pagans beat him, dragged him through the streets, and stoned him to death.

APPENDIX

WOMEN MARTYRED FOR THEIR FAITH IN JESUS

MARTYR	DEATH
AGATHA	Tortured by rods, hooks, the rack, and fire; rolled over coals and sharp, broken pieces of pottery.
AGNES	Committed herself to God; killed at the age of thirteen by the swift stroke of the executioner's axe.
ANASTASIA	Roman woman who disguised herself as a man to minister to Christians in jail; burned alive for her faith.
ANATOLIA	Refused to recant her faith and died from the sword.
BLANDINA	Repeatedly tortured and eventually trapped in a net; trampled by a bull.
CRISPINA	Said, "I have never sacrificed and I shall not do so, save to the one true God and to our Lord, Jesus Christ, his son!"[3] She was beheaded by governor of Rome.
CRISTINA	Her father, a Roman patrician, had her beaten and imprisoned at age twelve for refusing to sacrifice to a god. His successor ordered her tongue cut out and had her put in a dungeon with snakes. Bound to a tree, she was impaled with arrows.
DARIA	Put in a pit and buried alive with her fiancé.
EMERENTIAN	Foster-sister of Agnes, she was stoned to death while confronting pagans at Agnes's burial place.
EUGENIA	Left a life of privilege to enter a monastery; later beheaded for her faith.
EULALIA	Publicly gave a message about Christ; she was burned to death by flaming torches.
FELICITY	Pregnant slave who died with Perpetua, mauled in the arena and then killed by a gladiator; one of her guards became a Christian because of her.
LUCY	Sold her belongings and gave the money to the poor. She was arrested and brought before a judge, who commanded her to sacrifice to idols. She died from a sword through the neck.
PERPETUA	Noblewoman wounded by bulls in a Roman arena and killed by a young gladiator. Died for not worshiping Roman gods. She said, "I suffer what I'm suffering now, but then there will be another in me, who will suffer for me, because I am about to suffer for him."[4]

3. Early Christians, "Act of Martyrdom of St. Crispina."
4. Keiderling, "Perpetua."

APPENDIX

PETER'S WIFE	Executed by Roman authorities for her faith; just before Peter was crucified, he called to his wife and said, "Oh thou, remember the Lord."[5]
SAVINA	Helped Christians who were persecution by Diocletian; found praying at their tombs, she was martyred.
THECLA	Survived being burned at the stake, thrown to wild beasts, and drowned. She told her captors, "I am a daughter of Christ, Son of the living God. He alone is the Way, the Truth and the Life; He is the one who protects me."[6]
VALERIE	Refused to participate in a pagan festival; villagers beat her to death.

5. Miller, "Lesson from Peter's Wife."
6. Bowes, "St. Thecla."

BIBLIOGRAPHY

Barker, Joel A. "ChatGPT, AI and the 'Image of the Beast.'" *Christian Evidence* (blog), Jan. 19, 2023. https://www.christianevidence.net/2023/01/chatgpt-ai-and-image-of-beast.html.

Bible.org. "Probability of Prophecies Fulfilled." N.d. https://bible.org/illustration/probability-prophecies-fulfilled.

Bible Hub. "Symbolism of the Four Faces." N.d. https://biblehub.com/topical/s/symbolism_of_the_four_faces.htm.

———. "What Messiah did the Jews Expect?" n.d. https://biblehub.com/library/edersheim/the_life_and_times_of_jesus_the_messiah/chapter_v_what_messiah_did.htm.

Bowes, Peggy. "St. Thecla: Once, Twice, Three Times a (Lady) Martyr." Integrated Catholic Life, Sept. 23, 2010. https://integratedcatholiclife.org/2010/09/st-thecla-once-twice-three-times-a-lady-martyr/.

Calahan, John. "Is There Secular Evidence Herod Killed Babies Under the Age of Two?" *NeverThirsty* (blog), n.d. https://www.neverthirsty.org/bible-qa/qa-archives/question/is-there-secular-evidence-herod-killed-babies-under-the-age-of-two/.

Cole, Rachel. "10 Failed Doomsday Predictions." *Encyclopedia Britannica*, Apr. 3, 2013. https://www.britannica.com/list/10-failed-doomsday-predictions.

Dickerson, John S. "Clement of Rome." Jesus Skeptic, n.d. https://www.jesusskeptic.com/exist-clement.

Early Christians. "The Act of Martyrdom of St. Crispina." Mar. 8, 2014. https://www.earlychristians.org/the-act-of-martyrdom-of-st-crispina/.

Hibbard, Ray. "Predictions That Did Not Happen." *Edmond Life and Leisure*, Dec. 21, 2021. https://edmondlifeandleisure.com/predictions-that-did-not-happen-p22085-81.htm.

Josephus, Flavius. *The Works of Flavius Josephus*. Translated by William Whiston. Buffalo, NY: John E. Beardsley, 1895. Online edition. https://www.perseus.tufts.edu/hopper/text?doc=Perseus%3Atext%3A1999.01.0146%3Abook%3D18%3Asection%3D63.

Keiderling, Timothy J. "Perpetua." *Plough*, Aug. 3, 2023. https://www.plough.com/en/topics/faith/witness/perpetua.

Kirby, Peter, ed. "Cornelius Tacitus." Early Christian Writings, n.d. https://earlychristianwritings.com/tacitus.html.

BIBLIOGRAPHY

———. "First Clement." Translated by J. B. Lightfoot. Early Christian Writings, n.d. https://www.earlychristianwritings.com/text/1clement-lightfoot.html.

———. "Ignatius to the Smyrnaeans." Early Christian Writings, n.d. https://www.earlychristianwritings.com/text/ignatius-smyrnaeans-roberts.html.

Mayhew, Eugene J. "Alfred Edersheim—A Brief Biography." *Michigan Theological Journal* 2.2 (Fall 1991) 168. https://www.galaxie.com/article/mtj02-2-05.

McDowell, Sean. "Did the Apostles Really Die as Martyrs for Their Faith?" Christian Research Institute, Oct. 1, 2024. https://www.equip.org/articles/apostles-really-die-martyrs-faith/.

Miller, Sharon Hodde. "A Lesson from Peter's Wife." Aug. 2, 2011. https://sheworships.com/a-lesson-from-peters-wife/.

Polycarp. "The Epistle of Polycarp." Translated by J. B. Lightfoot. https://ccat.sas.upenn.edu/gopher/text/religion/churchwriters/ApostolicFathers/Polycarp#:~:text=Polycarp%202%3A1%20Wherefore%20gird%20up%20your%20loins%20and,His%20right%20hand%3B%20unto%20whom%20all%20things%20.

Reagan, David R. "Applying the Science of Probability to the Scriptures: Do Statistics Prove the Bible's Supernatural Origin?" Lamb and Lion Ministries, n.d. https://christinprophecy.org/articles/applying-the-science-of-probability-to-the-scriptures/.

Saint of the Day. "St. Andrew the Apostle: November 30." N.d. https://saintoftheday.com/st-andrew-the-apostle/.

Schmidt, Doug. "Fulfilled." The Wesleyan Church: Daily Devo, May 8, 2016. https://www.wesleyan.org/fulfilled-5013.

Scialdone, Tony. "Ox, Man, Lion, Eagle, the Compass, the Tribes and the Gospels." *GodWords: Theology and Other Stuff* (blog), n.d. https://godwords.org/ox-man-lion-eagle-the-compass-the-tribes-and-the-gospels/.

Sharefaith Team. "20 Christian Women Who Died as Martyrs." *Sharefaith Magazine*, n.d. https://blogrouting.sharefaith.com/2016/01/20-christian-woman-died-martyrs/.

Smollett, Tobias George. "Macrobius and the Slaughter of the Innocents." *Orthodox Christianity Then and Now* (blog), Dec. 29, 2012. https://www.johnsanidopoulos.com/2012/12/macrobius-and-slaughter-of-innocents.html.

Theologue. "Encyclopedia of Biblical Prophecy." Apr. 7, 2011. http://www.theologue.org/JBPayneEncyclopedia.htm.

United Church of God. "Beyond the Millennium." Dec. 22, 2010. https://www.ucg.org/learn/bible-study-aids/you-can-understand-bible-prophecy/you-can-understand-bible-prophecy/beyond.

www.ingramcontent.com/pod-product-compliance
Lightning Source LLC
Chambersburg PA
CBHW071825090426
42737CB00012B/2188